Paper Engineering & Pop-ups

FOR

DUMMIES®

by Rob Ives

Professional designer and paper engineer

WILEY

Wiley Publishing, Inc.

Paper Engineering & Pop-ups For Dummies®

Published by
Wiley Publishing, Inc.
111 River St.
Hoboken, NJ 07030-5774
www.wiley.com

WILEY

About the Author

Rob Ives is a full-time designer and paper engineer. He has had a number of books published on the subject, but he spends most of his work time running his paper automata Web site at www.flying-pig.co.uk.

Rob started his career as a primary school teacher, but gradually his enthusiasm for paper engineering took over, and finally in year 2000 he left teaching and began work as a self-employed designer. Since then, he has returned to schools and colleges to give talks and run workshops.

Rob lives in Cumbria in the UK with his wife Pauline and his two children, Martha and Elliot.

Dedication

This book is dedicated to Pauline, Martha, and Elliot — the lights of my life.

Author's Acknowledgments

Thanks to all the people at Wiley Publishing who have helped with this project. It has been a fascinating process, and I have appreciated the help and support all the way through.

A special thank you goes to Chad Sievers, my project editor, who has been so helpful and supportive throughout the project. He has been a calm and reassuring voice in the teeth of rewrites, edits, loads and loads of artwork, and looming deadlines! Thanks to Danielle Voirol, whose help with editing has been invaluable and much appreciated. Thanks also to Michael Lewis, the acquisitions editor, without whom none of this would have been possible. Literally!

Thanks also to Miranda Caroligne for her enthusiastic help in the early stages of this project. Finally, thanks to my family for all their patience and support as I once again disappeared to the word processor.

Publisher's Acknowledgments

We're proud of this book; please send us your comments through our Dummies online registration form located at `http://dummies.custhelp.com`. For other comments, please contact our Customer Care Department within the U.S. at 877-762-2974, outside the U.S. at 317-572-3993, or fax 317-572-4002.

Some of the people who helped bring this book to market include the following:

Acquisitions, Editorial, and Media Development

Project Editor: Chad R. Sievers

Acquisitions Editor: Michael Lewis

Senior Copy Editor: Danielle Voirol

Assistant Editor: Erin Calligan Mooney

Editorial Program Coordinator: Joe Niesen

Technical Editor: Paul Jackson

Editorial Reviewer: Miranda Caroligne

Editorial Manager: Michelle Hacker

Editorial Assistant: Jennette ElNaggar

Cover Photos: © Rob Ives/Flying Pig

Cartoons: Rich Tennant (www.the5thwave.com)

Composition Services

Project Coordinator: Patrick Redmond

Layout and Graphics: Carl Byers, Reuben W. Davis, Nikki Gately, Melissa Jester

Proofreaders: Betty Kish, Dwight Ramsey

Indexer: Broccoli Information Management

Publishing and Editorial for Consumer Dummies

Diane Graves Steele, Vice President and Publisher, Consumer Dummies

Kristin Ferguson-Wagstaffe, Product Development Director, Consumer Dummies

Ensley Eikenburg, Associate Publisher, Travel

Kelly Regan, Editorial Director, Travel

Publishing for Technology Dummies

Andy Cummings, Vice President and Publisher, Dummies Technology/General User

Composition Services

Gerry Fahey, Vice President of Production Services

Debbie Stailey, Director of Composition Services

Contents at a Glance

Table of Contents

Introduction

• •

Don't let paper fool you — it isn't just for drawing and writing. Paper is flexible and easy to cut, and it can be surprisingly strong when you fold it. Those qualities make paper a great building material for all kinds of art projects. And yes, you can still decorate the surface of your paper projects, even though a lot of them look good in white.

Paper engineering and making pop-ups are hobbies that anyone can take part in — from schoolchildren to retired people, from the businessman who wants a relaxing, creative project to work on in the evenings to the schoolteacher who wants a hobby she can share with her pupils. The skills are easy to pick up, and the tools you need are inexpensive and easy to get hold of.

Using some simple techniques, you can express your creative side by making these delightful paper creations, and when you're done, you have the pleasure of sharing the fruits of your creativity with your family and friends. Building on these skills, you can soon have the ability to design and make your own pop-up and paper-engineering projects.

About This Book

My aim in writing this book is to share my love of paper engineering with you and to show you just how easy and rewarding it is to take up this fascinating pastime. Although I tell you how to add color and embellishments to your projects, the focus is on putting paper together in creative ways. This book introduces all the major aspects of paper engineering, including making simple pop-up cards, designing storybooks using pop-ups, and making animated paper models. You can find info on basic concepts and techniques, along with complete projects with step-by-step instructions. I also discuss the design process itself, from seeking inspiration and getting your ideas down on paper to making the transition from sketch to completed model.

This book offers you, the beginning paper engineer, a chance to get your feet wet. I introduce many different types of paper engineering and present basic projects for most types. As you become more familiar and comfortable with working with paper, you may want to try more advanced and different types of projects. I suggest you look on the Web and at other books for inspiration.

You can read this book from start to finish, but you don't have to. I designed *Paper Engineering & Pop-ups For Dummies* so you can start with whatever project or technique interests you most. If you need extra information, just follow the cross-references.

Conventions Used in This Book

To help you find your way around this book, I use the following conventions:

- ✔ I use *italics* to emphasize words and to highlight new terms or words that I define.

- ✔ **Bold** indicates the action part of numbered steps or the keywords in a bulleted list.

- ✔ `Monofont` is for Web addresses. Note that when this book was printed, some Web addresses may have needed to break across two lines of text. If that happened, rest assured that I haven't put in any extra characters (such as hyphens) to indicate the break. Just type in exactly what you see in this book, ignoring the line break.

- ✔ All measurements in this book are marked in inches. Most of the diagrams include the inch symbol ("), but for those that don't, you can safely assume that inches are being used.

- ✔ In the figures, I use the following symbols:

  - • **Dotted or dashed lines:** Score lines, where you fold the paper
  - • **Solid lines:** Cut lines
  - • **Gray area:** Where to glue

- ✔ Unless otherwise stated, all card/paper in the projects is A4 or letter size (8½" x 11") and has 230 micron (9 thousandths of an inch) thickness. For more on paper thickness, see Chapter 2.

What You're Not to Read

You don't need to read some parts of this book. *Sidebars,* the areas of text on a gray background, are there to add a little background information, perhaps a little color or an interesting anecdote to do with the subject being discussed, but they're not vital to your understanding of the subject.

Foolish Assumptions

I've made a few assumptions while writing this book. These assumptions can help smooth the way as I pass my enthusiasm for paper engineering on to you. I've assumed the following — I hope it's not too foolish!

- ✔ You're interested in paper engineering and pop-ups and want to be able to make and possibly design your own pieces.

- ✔ You're willing to spend a small amount of money buying some simple tools, such as scissors and a cutting mat.

- ✔ You have a few basic skills, such as the ability to measure and cut accurately. (Don't worry too much about this, because I help you with some more specialized cutting skills in the book.)

How This Book Is Organized

I organize this book into five parts. The first four deal with different aspects of paper engineering, and the fifth part is a *For Dummies* staple. Here's a preview.

Part I: Introducing the Magic of Paper Engineering

If you're new to paper engineering, you want to start right here. This part has four chapters that give an overview on all aspects of the subject. I give you the lowdown on just what paper engineering is. I talk about paper and card and give you some guidelines on setting up your own paper-engineering workshop. The part finishes off with a chapter on how to use the tools of the trade safely and effectively.

Part II: Going Flat Out: Commencing with Creative Paper Crafts

This part helps you get down to making some projects that are flat or can fold flat. It starts with some simple but effective paper-engineering crafts, including greeting cards that you can make for your friends, and moves on to introduce you to making pop-up cards using a whole variety of techniques. The final chapters in this part show you how to make other pop-up and pull-tab mechanisms and how to string several pages together into a book. Don't worry — I offer you loads of hands-on projects and plenty of illustrations to help you on your way.

Part III: Paper Sculpture and Animation: Adding Some 3D Life to Paper

This part covers paper sculpture and shows how you can fold, cut, and crease paper into fun 3D designs. This part also introduces the concept of paper automata, the fascinating world where models come to life through some simple mechanisms. Using plenty of projects, I go through the basics of paper automata. You get tips on using cams, levers, other mechanisms, and linkages, along with advice on making sure everything fits together.

Part IV: Drafting Your Own Designs and Creations

In this part, I show you the best ways of coming up with ideas and how to take these ideas from sketches to the finished model. I show you how color can enhance your designs and how to make fantastic paper models you can be proud of. I also show you how computers can help you with your paper engineering, including a section on free software you can easily use. And to round everything out, I talk a little about how you can make some extra money from your new hobby.

Part V: The Part of Tens

No *For Dummies* book would be complete without a Part of Tens. In this part, I go through ten helpful hints for making the best of your paper engineering and give you ten tips on designing and varying models.

Icons Used in This Book

In the margins of *Paper Engineering & Pop-ups For Dummies* (as in all *For Dummies* books), you see icons to help you find your way through the text. Here's what those icons mean:

This icon points out ideas and techniques that can make your project a bit easier.

Some techniques you need over and over. They're marked with the Remember icon. Take note of the techniques this icon highlights.

Be careful! This icon helps you avoid hurting yourself, damaging your equipment, or messing up your project. Keep an eye out for this one; it'll save you time, money, and possible injury.

Where to Go from Here

I always like to start with the hands-on stuff, so you may want to grab a pair of scissors and a ruler and head for one of the many projects in this book. If you like greeting cards, you may like to start in Chapter 5 with one of the simple projects. If you're interested in making moving models (paper automata), then head straight for Chapter 10. Those of you with a more artistic leaning may be more interested in making a paper sculpture. If so, go to Chapter 9. Just check out the table of contents or the index for a topic that interests you and flip to that chapter. You can jump in wherever you like and jump about from section to section. Of course, if you're new to paper engineering, I recommend that you at least read through Chapter 4 before you start the projects so you get a good grasp on safety and techniques.

Or you can just start at the very beginning and read your way from cover to cover. No matter where you start, have a piece of paper and some scissors handy and get ready to dive right in.

Part I

Introducing the Magic of Paper Engineering

"Okay Kids. Today we'll be working on picking the best color of paper, creasing paper, and using a glue gun safely."

Part I
Introducing the Magic of Paper Engineering

In this part . . .

Welcome aboard! Here you go into the wonderful world of paper. In this part, I introduce the basics of paper engineering and outline some of the aspects that this book covers, from pop-ups and pull tabs to paper sculptures and animations. I also highlight the different types of paper you can use with your creations. I then guide you through setting up your paper-engineering workshop and stocking it with tools and materials. Finally, this part wraps up with advice on making your paper project and with some safety rules.

Chapter 1

Unfolding the Mystery of Paper Engineering

In This Chapter

▶ Looking at pop-ups and pull tabs

▶ Going artistic with paper sculpture

▶ Creating paper animations

Whoever came up with the idea of *construction* paper had the right idea: Paper makes a great building material — you can easily fold, bend, tear, and cut it, and sticking the parts together requires nothing more than a bit of glue. In elementary school, you may have been a bit haphazard about putting stuff together. Now that you're (somewhat) grown up, you don't have to be any less creative, but you can do a lot more with paper when you play engineer and plan ahead.

Paper engineering basically means cutting and creating shapes with paper or card. With paper engineering, you can make pop-up and moving cards, and you can create elegant and sophisticated sculptures using interesting 3D shapes. You can even make fully working machines that use only paper for their mechanisms.

This chapter gives you an overview of the main types of paper engineering that I focus on in this book. You discover how pop-ups and pull tabs are made and how they work. I take a look at paper sculpture, a way of using the paper itself as the art medium rather than just using it as the place where the art is drawn. I also introduce you to paper animations, or *automata,* which are a kind of humorous machine that shows a short animated scene made entirely out of paper. (*Note:* If you get the basics down and want to try your hand at design, I can help you out there, too — simply check out Part IV of this book.)

Including the Right Supplies in Your Workplace

Paper engineering is a relatively inexpensive hobby. You need only a few tools and materials to get started. Here's a list of the tools and materials you need to take the first steps (check out Chapter 3 for details about these items and other items you may want to add to your workspace later):

✔ Scissors

✔ Sharp craft knife

✔ Self-healing cutting mat

- ✔ Ruler
- ✔ White school glue (and glue spreader)
- ✔ Glue stick
- ✔ A range of different types of paper and card stock

Using colored papers and different textures can all add to the final effect. From corrugated cardboard to homemade paper, and from embossed or textured papers to foil-coated, reflective card stock — all these materials are an inspiration to the paper artist. You can combine them for a fantastic effect. For example, you can use corrugated cardboard to make the texture of a tree trunk reflecting in a pond made from blue foil-coated card. See Figure 1-1 for an example that incorporates different paper types.

Figure 1-1:
Textured paper adds interest to a relatively flat project.

Flip to Chapter 2 for more on paper and to Chapter 3 for advice on tools, materials, and setting up your workspace. Of course, tools and materials don't do much good if you don't know how to use them, so check out Chapter 4 for some info on cutting and construction techniques.

Cutting Away with Cutout Greeting Cards

When you cut a shape out of a piece of paper, sometimes you're after the piece you just cut out. And sometimes you're after the leftover scraps, wanting to let the hole do the work for you. Artists can give you a neat, technical discussion of positive and negative space, but for the paper engineer, the important idea is this: Cutouts can make great greeting cards. See Figure 1-2 for a sample where you cut out the word "Wow!" and use a different colored paper directly behind the cutout.

Instead of adding colors or paints, *cutout cards* use holes and cuts as their main decorations. Through the holes and cuts, you can see other paper of other colors or just an interesting shadow. You can make cutout cards with a craft knife using a whole variety of different weights and colors of card. Chapter 5 gives you several opportunities to make your own cutout cards.

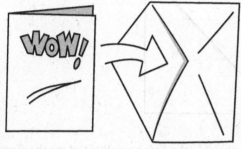

Figure 1-2:
A sample
cutout card.

Rising to the Occasion with Pop-ups

Pop-ups literally add a whole new dimension to books and greeting cards. Pop-ups use clever folds of paper to make ingenious mechanisms. When viewers open pop-up pages, anything can happen. You can open a greeting card and find that an entire 3D scene — complete with castles, knights, and a dragon — comes into view. Open another card, and a whole bunch of flowers appears like a magic trick. Even simple pop-ups can be surprisingly effective. This section gives you a quick overview of pop-ups. Check out Chapters 6 and 8 for more in-depth info.

Looking at how pop-ups pop up

With a pop-up, you open the page of the pop-up book (or card), and the character lifts into view. In the simplest pop-ups, you make the effect easily. A cutout of the character is fixed so that it sits just in front of the background. By clever use of paper tabs, the character folds flat when you close the book or card. Figure 1-3 shows an example of a simple pop-up card. The shadows cast on the background give the flat character dimension.

You can make more-complicated pop-ups by changing the way parts are folded and how the characters join together. If the fold and tabs that hold the card together are angled, then when the card opens, the character twists into position instead of just lifting straight up. Figure 1-4 shows how a character can swivel into view.

Even the most complicated pop-ups work using the same small set of mechanisms. When you understand these mechanisms, you can design your own amazing paper inventions.

Eyeing the different pop-up methods

Pop-ups come in all shapes and sizes. They use a variety of different mechanisms to do their popping. From the coffee-table books to greeting cards, each pop-up may use a single mechanism or a whole range of linked mechanisms. Read on to find out more about the types of pop-ups just waiting for your discovery:

- ✔ **Parallel pop-ups:** You may well have made the simplest type of parallel pop-up when you were at school. Usually, parallel pop-ups open only halfway so that the book or card is opened to 90 degrees. In front of the background of the card is one or more layers of pictures that are parallel to it. Figure 1-5 shows a typical parallel pop-up.

  From this simple starting point, you can change and add to parallel pop-ups to make quite sophisticated pictures with very interesting mechanisms. With care, the movement of the picture as the card opens can really add to the project's impact.

- ✔ **Pop-out pop-ups:** The second common type of pop-up is the pop-out pop-up, which you most commonly see in books. With pop-out pop-ups, the pages open fully, and a 3D model appears miraculously in the middle of the page.

  You can make fantastically complicated pop-out pop-ups that still fold flat, hiding their secrets within. Figure 1-6 shows an example from *Encyclopedia Prehistorica Dinosaurs: The Definitive Pop-Up,* by Robert Sabuda and Matthew Reinhart (Candlewick).

Figure 1-5:
A parallel
pop-up cat.

Figure 1-6: An incredible pop-out pop-up dinosaur.

Chapter 6 explains how to make both kinds of pop-ups.

What you can do with pop-ups

Pop-up designers are always looking to push the limits of paper engineering. Look through some of the pop-up books in your local bookstore, and you'll be amazed at what people have achieved. Open the page, and a ship — complete with masts and sails — heaves into view over stormy seas. Turn the page, and a castle magically appears before your eyes. Figure 1-7, from *The Christmas Alphabet: Deluxe Anniversary Edition,* by Robert Sabuda (Orchard Books), shows the kind of effect you can create with pop-up scenes.

Of course, pop-ups aren't just for children's books. Authors and paper engineers have made all kinds of pop-up books for grown-ups, including lavishly illustrated books of plants and animals and even pop-up graphic novels. (*Note:* That's *graphic* as in visual arts, not how vivid and realistic the details are. A *graphic novel* — a handy term if you don't want to admit to reading comic books — is a bound book in comic-strip format.)

The surprise and delight of the movement also makes pop-ups ideal for all kinds of paper projects. Pop-up greeting cards are expensive to buy from a card shop because they need to be hand-assembled. But a homemade, home-designed card costs you nothing more than the modest material costs and a wee bit of your elbow grease. The fact they're homemade and individually designed makes them all the more delightful to the recipient! With care, you can even design business cards with pop-ups inside them. See Figure 1-8 for an example of a pop-up business card.

Figure 1-7:
A beautiful
paper dove
appears
when the
card opens.

Used with permission from Robert Sabuda

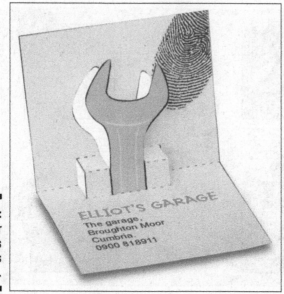

Figure 1-8:
Make your
business
cards
pop up.

Moving Pictures: Pull Tabs and Wheels

Pull tabs, wheels, and other ways of making part of a picture move are so often part of pop-up books that many people call all these mechanisms "pop-ups." But these pictures usually don't pop up, strictly speaking. Flat mechanisms rotate or slide a printed picture or piece of card across the page.

Each image in a pull-tab picture has one or more tabs. As the name implies, *pull tabs* are little strips of card, usually at the side of the picture, that you grab hold of and pull gently. As you pull, some sort of action takes place on the card — a piece rotates, slides, or jumps up from the page. For example, a penguin may jump into the sea, or a whale may dive beneath the waves. Pull the tabs, and magic happens.

Moving-picture books also use *paper wheels*. Often, these wheels, which are like giant washers, are mostly hidden within the page. Just grab the edge of the wheel and turn it, and you can see the picture change through a small hole in the page. You may see wheels that make a star twinkle or eyes move.

All kinds of moving pictures are possible. See Figure 1-9 for an example of a moving picture, and check out Chapters 7 and 8 for some pull-tab and wheel projects.

Figure 1-9:
Pulling the tab puts the workers in motion.

Used with permission from Castle: Medieval Days and Knights, by Kyle Olman

Going 3D with Paper Sculpture

Fold a crease here and a curve of paper there; mix some interesting paper shapes and colors, and soon you've created an amazing paper sculpture. Artists of all kinds have experimented with paper as a 3D medium. They've produced paper art from the abstract to the representative, from the tiny to the enormous. The results can be fabulous. The simple flowing form of the paper surface combined with the texture of the surface can make wondrous art pieces.

This section gives you the lowdown on how you can make 3D sculptures with paper. You can check out Chapter 9 for more in-depth information and several projects you can try.

Focusing on basic paper sculpture

Instead of paint or pencil, paper sculpture uses creases and cuts, light and shadow to create shapes for artistic effect. These sculptures can be freestanding, or they may be attached to a background and mounted on a wall. Figure 1-10 shows an example of paper sculpture.

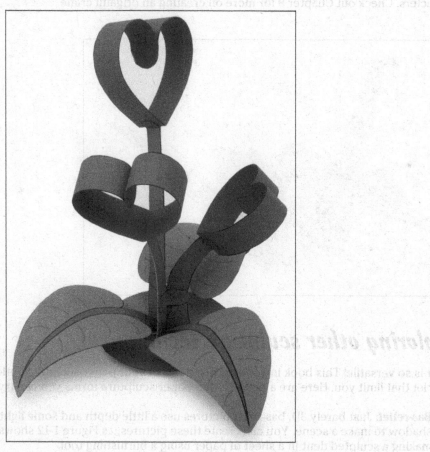

Figure 1-10:
A freestanding paper sculpture.

Paper engineers use a whole range of interesting techniques with paper sculpture. Special score lines, in which you use the point of a pair of scissors to make a dent in a piece of paper, can help you fold a curved 3D shape. You can curl paper by running it over a pen or pencil. And a number of creative folds — or the strategic application of glue — can transform a simple sheet of paper into a gallery-worthy (or at least mantel-worthy) masterpiece.

Folding paper Japanese-style

When people hear about paper modeling, one of the first things they think of is origami. Origami is a special case of paper sculpture. The word *origami* comes from Japanese words meaning "folding paper." To fit with the modern definition of origami, the model must be made from a single square of paper with no cuts.

Even with these restrictions, all kinds of models are possible, from the traditional crane (as in Figure 1-11) to incredibly detailed models. Some modelers even work to themes. For instance, you can find Star Wars origami designs and designs based on popular comic book characters. Check out Chapter 9 for more on creating an origami crane.

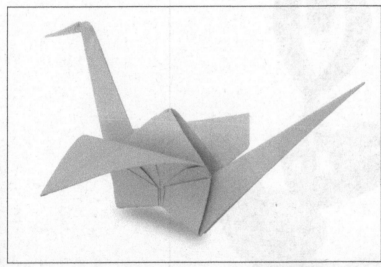

Figure 1-11: The traditional origami crane.

Exploring other sculpture techniques

Paper is so versatile! This book introduces just a few of your paper-sculpting options, but don't let that limit you. Here are a couple other paper sculpture forms you can try:

- **Bas-relief:** Just barely 3D, bas-relief pictures use a little depth and some light and shadow to make a scene. You can create these pictures, as Figure 1-12 shows, by making a sculpted dent in a sheet of paper using a burnishing tool.

- **The long cut:** Some paper artists specialize in making 3D sculptures from a single sheet of paper. They use sharp craft knives to make cuts in the paper and then fold up and arrange the pieces to make a sculpture. This results in a subject that appears to grow out of the paper. Using this technique, artists such as Peter Callesen (www. petercallesen.com) create amazing paper art, such as a sheet of paper that looks like a vast empty scene with a ruined building looming from the center. See Figure 1-13 for an example of a single-sheet model.

Figure 1-12: A bas-relief paper picture.

Figure 1-13: A long-cut spider rises out of a flat piece of paper.

Bringing Paper to Life with Paper Animations

For many hundreds of years, talented artisans have tried to create the illusion of life. They designed and built machines — powered by clockwork or by the turn of a handle — that could imitate living things. Usually, these models, known as *automata,* would play a short scene over and over to the delight of the onlooker.

Traditional automata were usually made from wood, leather, and brass, but paper engineers love a challenge. Today, paper engineers create all kinds of intricate and amazing models from paper and card using paper levers and paper cams. For instance, paper pigs really can fly! Figure 1-14 shows a paper animation model that uses a crank to make the pig move. The wings are attached to the box top so that they flap as the pig moves up and down.

This section gives you an overview of paper animations, including the types of creations you can make. Flip to Chapters 10 through 12 for more in-depth info.

Automata through the ages

Through the ages, automata makers have amazed people with their skills. Automata in the temple would impress worshippers in Ancient Greek times. A moving statue of Athena, goddess of wisdom and war, would certainly encourage donations to the temple funds! The more impressive and lifelike the statue, the more generous the worshippers would be.

Even the great Leonardo da Vinci tried his hand at automata design back in the 15th century. In notebooks rediscovered in the 1950s, Leonardo had drawn designs for a robot-type automaton that could move its arms, sit down in a chair, and stand back up again.

In the 16th century, the French engineer Jacques de Vaucanson created an automaton that could play the flute; supposedly it could play 12 different songs. He even created a mechanical duck that could eat corn and then poop!

Figure 1-14:
Making
a pig fly
with paper.

Checking out the characteristics of paper animations

You can make all kinds of paper animations, or automata, by cleverly combining some basic mechanisms. These basic mechanisms include the following:

- ✔ **Cam:** A *cam* is an irregularly shaped piece fitted to a shaft or axle. When it turns, it pushes against another part, the cam follower, and moves it up and down.

- ✔ **Crank:** A *crank* (part of the crank-slider mechanism in Chapter 12) is the part that drives a piston up and down in a car engine. In paper animations, cranks likewise move parts up and down, sometimes in a circular path.

For example, a crank may move a surfboard, or a cam may make a bird peck. You can also create other paper mechanisms, such as gears and lever systems. In paper animations, all the parts are made from paper and they work together to tell the final story.

Most of the time you encounter paper animations, you find them in kits. A typical kit has several sheets of parts printed onto heavy paper or card, along with an instruction sheet. From there, creating your project is just a matter of cutting the parts out and gluing them together. Figure 1-15 shows a paper *Tyrannosaurus rex* from a kit I designed. This model uses different mechanisms to make the *T. rex* reach down and grab the hapless caveman.

With the projects in this book, I provide you with step-by-step instructions to create your own parts and make your own creations. Check out Chapters 10 through 12 for several different projects.

Figure 1-15:
A paper
T. rex.

Making moving parts

By itself, a sheet of paper isn't strong. However, you can make it quite strong by simply shaping the paper into tubes and box sections. Easy as that! From paper, you can create cranks, levers, and more. It's even possible to create gears, although they aren't as easy to make as the gears in traditional automata models. (Check out Figure 1-16 for an example of moving hens.)

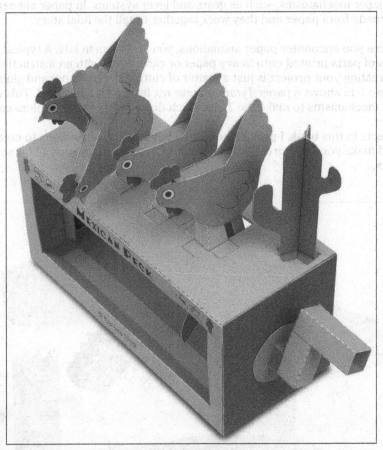

Figure 1-16:
Hens go up
and down.

Some designs work better than others, and inevitably paper does have its limitations. Some mechanisms are hard to construct using paper only. You just can't do certain things with paper because of its light weight and its tendency to fold, tear, or bend. However, you can use other items to get around the limitations. For example, some paper animations use a coin, string, pieces of dowel, and other items to help the mechanism work.

However, in my humble paper-engineering opinion, the best models use only paper. I sometimes use coins, but I try to avoid other nonpaper materials. The coiled spring is very useful in traditional automata design, but unfortunately, it's very difficult to replace in paper models; often, you have to replace springs with weights as a way of storing energy. Chapter 11 helps you build strong, moving parts with paper and explains how to use coins as weights.

Chapter 2

Paper — The Essential Ingredient

- -

In This Chapter

▶ Deciding on the right type of paper for the job

▶ Shopping for your paper needs

▶ Being good to the environment

- -

On the list of the most important inventions of all time, paper is surely near the top of the list. With the development of writing, paper was the perfect place to record everything from love notes to treaty declarations without the tedious use of hammer and chisel. The Chinese invented the first paper around 100 CE; however, the Egyptians were the ones who gave paper its modern name. They shredded the stems of the *papyrus* plant, which grew on the shores of the Nile, into fibers and beat it flat; when dried, it worked as a writing surface.

If you've ever stepped foot into a crafts or office supply store, you're well aware of the immense variety of paper created since the Ancient Egyptian Era. Most papers are still made in basically the same way. However, today you have much more to choose from. People can now create paper from all sorts of plant fibers, trees (wood pulp), and recycled existing-paper products, as well as plant-based textiles such as cotton and linen (and even semi-digested plant fibers from elephant dung!). Changing these starting materials, as well as the paper thickness and finish, brings paper production from crude to utterly creative — and paper engineers get to reap the rewards.

This chapter gives you an overview of the basic types of paper available for you as you create your paper-engineering projects. Here, I also help you shop and find the paper, and I include some ways to be friendly to the environment.

Choosing the Right Paper (or Card): Reams of Possibilities

As you plan to make your next (or even your first) paper-engineering project, choosing the right paper for the project is important. Which type of paper do you use? Thick or thin? Stiff or flexible? Glossy or matte? The paper you select is often essential to ensuring your project stands strong and doesn't flop.

Paper and card come in all sorts of different types. In fact, you can find a paper type in a whole range of different thicknesses and colors. When you're choosing the paper for your latest project, you need to know what you're looking for. Paper that's too weak doesn't work properly in paper mechanisms, and paper that's too stiff doesn't work well for paper hinges. In this section, I discuss paper types, weights, and finishes and have a quick look at some of the more exotic materials.

You often hear the word *card* when considering all the possibilities for paper. The difference between paper and card isn't so easy to define. The words are almost interchangeable. Usually, the difference is simply a matter of weight: As a general rule, card is stiff and thick, and paper is flexible and thin. But here's an important question to ask: Are you doing paper engineering or cardboard engineering? (I usually say *paper engineering* because I think it sounds classier, but you can definitely find cardboard artists out there who disagree.)

Paper types

Paper comes in a fantastic range of types. *Paper type* is defined by a combination of properties, including the fineness of the paper fibers, the stiffness of the paper, the texture of the surface, and the overall thickness of each sheet. Luckily, picking the right paper isn't as daunting as you may think. Many papers, as long as they're relatively strong and stiff, are perfectly suitable for paper engineering and the projects in this book. Here's a selection of some of the common types of paper you may come across:

- ✔ **Art paper:** Also referred to as *art board*, this smooth-finish paper is coated in china clay to fill in any imperfections. This paper can have a matte or glossy finish. (For more on types of finishes, refer to the "Paper finishes" section later in this chapter.)

- ✔ **Bond paper:** This is a high-quality smooth paper used mainly for stationery and letterheads. Bond paper was originally used for printing bonds and certificates.

- ✔ **Acid-free paper:** Most paper is slightly acidic. Over time, the natural acids within the paper turn it yellow and brittle. Pick up an old paperback book in a secondhand book shop, and you can see the effect for yourself.

Use acid-free paper when it's important for the paper to last. Acid-free paper is expensive, but it lasts for hundreds of years.

- ✔ **Newsprint:** If you can't tell by the name, newsprint is the paper your newspapers are made from. This cheap, uncoated paper is often made using recycled paper fiber. It has a very high acid content, so it becomes yellow and brittle very quickly, especially when exposed to sunlight. You can use it for sketching, but it generally isn't suitable for paper engineering.

- ✔ **Pulp board:** Available in a range of thicknesses, pulp board is general-purpose card that has a smooth finish. It has an absorbent surface, so you can glue it with solvent-free glues, such as white school glue.

Pulp board is great for most paper-engineering projects. The main workhorse that I use for most of my work is 230-micron pulp board (about 9 thousandths of an inch — I discuss paper thickness in the next section). In fact, except where I state otherwise, it's the paper I use for all the projects in this book. I tend to buy pulp board in packages of 1,000 sheets and then buy only a few ten-packs of other paper for more decorative work.

- ✔ **Laid paper:** This is a textured paper, often used as a high-quality writing paper. While the pulp is still slightly wet, the paper mill adds textures to the paper using a special textured roller called a *dandy roller.*

- ✔ **Photo paper:** This paper is specially designed to print out photographs on your home inkjet printer. Photo paper often has a coating on only one side, so make sure you put it in the printer the right way up.

Paper weight and thickness

Although many paper pros refer to a paper's heaviness as *paper thickness,* most people describe papers by weight. Knowing a paper's weight is important because the thickness of the paper is the feature that most defines its stiffness.

Finding the weight of a piece of paper can be tricky if you don't have the original packaging. I keep a few samples in my toolbox with the weight written on them so that I can compare them. I then compare them by touch; feeling works much better than looking.

Although you can measure paper weight or thickness in loads of different ways, here are the three biggies:

✔ **Basis weight:** Also known as *poundage,* basis weight is the system used in the United States. Instead of being based on a single sheet of paper, the basis weight is the weight of an entire ream of paper. A *ream* is usually 500 sheets of paper (but it can range from 480 to 516 sheets per ream). For example, a ream of 500 sheets of photocopy paper weighs 20 pounds. Therefore, photocopy paper is described as 20-pound paper, which is sometimes written as 20#.

To make things even more complicated, the size of the paper being weighed changes from type to type. For example, photocopy paper is usually 17" x 22", whereas newsprint is 24" x 36". Comparing basis weights between different types of paper is difficult. Luckily, you don't need to do that very often.

✔ **Grammage:** Used mainly in Europe and almost every other country except for the United States, *grammage* is the weight (or mass) of a single sheet of paper with the dimensions of 1 meter by 1 meter (a square approximately 39 inches on a side). Regular photocopy paper is usually around 80 grams per square meter. This is written as either 80 gsm or, more usually, 80 g/m².

✔ **Caliper thickness:** Finally! A measure of the actual thickness of a single sheet of paper. Caliper thickness is the measure of thickness of the paper using — not surprisingly — a set of *calipers* (check out Chapter 4 for info on including calipers in your toolbox). The thickness is measured in thousandths of an inch in the United States or in microns in the rest of the world. To convert from microns to thousandths of an inch, divide by 25.4.

For most paper-engineering work, caliper thickness is the most useful measurement. The paper weight can give you a rough idea of the thickness, but just because a paper is heavier doesn't mean it's thicker. The only way to find the thickest or thinnest papers out of a stack is to actually measure them.

Grammage and basis weight deal with mass in terms of the length and width of the paper. If you have two sheets of paper with the same length and width and the same mass, their thicknesses can differ if one is denser than the other. *Density* is the weight divided by volume. In other words, think about the weight difference of a Styrofoam block versus a cement block of the same size. The same difference occurs with paper, although maybe not quite that extreme.

Comparing basis weight, grammage, and thickness can be a challenge, but I include a table in the Cheat Sheet at the front of this book that you can use to estimate paper thickness when you're at the store.

Paper size

The United States and Canada measure paper in a set of standard sizes. The most common sizes include letter, legal, ledger, and tabloid. Table 2-1 shows the dimensions of these common sizes in inches and millimeters.

Table 2-1	Converting Standard Paper Sizes	
Name	*Size in Inches*	*Size in Millimeters*
Letter	8.5 x 11	216 x 279
Legal	8.5 x 14	216 x 356
Ledger	17 x 11	432 x 279
Tabloid	11 x 17	279 x 432

In other parts of the world, paper comes in the International Organization for Standardization (ISO) 216 sizes, often called *A sizes*. In this system, each size has half the area of the preceding size. The higher the number, the smaller the paper. Table 2-2 shows this comparison.

Table 2-2	Converting ISO Paper Sizes	
Name	*Size in Inches*	*Size in Millimeters*
A2	16.5 x 23.4	420 x 594
A3	11.7 x 16.5	297 x 420
A4	8.3 x 11.7	210 x 297
A5	5.8 x 8.3	148 x 210

Letter size and A4 size are very close together, and A3 and ledger/tabloid size are almost equivalent. Unless otherwise stated, the sheets of paper I use in the projects in this book are A4 or letter size.

Paper finishes

When you begin shopping for paper (see the later section "Shopping Smart: Where to Find Paper and Embellishments"), you may be amazed at the selection. I love to visit our local craft store and revel in the wondrous variety of papers. The store carries everything from perfectly smooth, glossy art board to the work of local craftspeople: handmade papers that have all sorts of threads, glitter, and even skeleton leaves woven right into the paper. You can find a type of paper finish to suit every occasion and every project you want to make.

A paper's *finish* is simply the quality or texture of the surface. Picking the right finish is important; the different finishes add an extra dimension to your paper in the same way that color does. Pick the texture that suits the project you're working on.

Paper producers make textures in a few different ways:

✔ **Rough:** You get a rough texture simply by leaving the paper raw instead of smoothing it off during the manufacturing process. Sometimes producers give the paper even more texture by running it through textured rollers either before or after it's dried.

✔ **Smooth:** On the flip side, smooth papers are often coated in a thin layer of china clay. This fills in the gaps between the fibers and has the added advantage of whitening the paper.

✔ **Gloss:** The paper is coated and then rolled between two glossy rollers while still wet. The end result is a shiny, high-gloss finish.

✔ **Matte:** Without the glossy treatment, papers have a flat, nonreflective surface.

Wove, or smooth finish, is the best for most of the moving parts of paper mechanisms, but you can use textured papers to give the rest of your model an interesting look.

Figure 2-1 shows a variety of different paper textures available today.

Figure 2-1:
Various
paper
textures.

Exotic materials: More than just paper

Besides the normal papers you can find at your local craft store, look for a whole variety of paper and card that really begins to stretch the definition of what paper is. Give these more exotic papers a go around in your paper-engineering projects:

✔ **Metalized paper:** This type is made using an ordinary sheet of paper. On one surface, a microscopically thin layer of metalized plastic film is bonded into place. The result is a type of paper that you can use like ordinary paper, but it has a metallic finish. These papers come in a variety of colors and are even available with a holographic finish. They're fun to experiment with and can give some fabulous decorative results.

Metalized papers are coated in a waterproof film, so you need to use solvent-based glues to stick them. (See Chapter 3 for more on glue types.)

✔ **Foam board:** Foam board is a layer of plastic foam about ⅛" thick with paper bonded onto both faces. Foam board is light, stiff, and more expensive than paper or card, but it's fun for making architectural models as well as large-scale pop-up cards. My son and I recently made a fantastic fortress using foam board. It's a very versatile material.

- ✔ **Corrugated cardboard:** Okay, corrugated cardboard isn't exactly exotic, but when you want to make big projects that need heavy-duty materials, you may find yourself scrounging through the wilds of your closet or garage for old cardboard boxes.

- ✔ **Precolored papers:** A whole variety of different colored papers can make perfect additions to the paper engineer's workshop. Both paper and card are available in a variety of solid colors, as well as preprinted patterns and graduated color changes. Combining these pro papers can make your paper-engineering projects look even more fantastic. See Figure 2-2 for some patterns.

Of course, you can also color your own paper using watercolor paint or marbling ink. See Chapter 4 for some paper-coloring techniques.

Figure 2-2:
A variety of preprinted papers.

Shopping Smart: Where to Find Paper and Embellishments

Shopping for paper and embellishments with a keen eye can make your projects unique as well as keep your wallet in good standing. If you want to find unique paper and accessories, you have several options, particularly if you're on a budget. This section presents some of my suggestions.

Relying on arts and crafts shops

Your local arts and crafts store can be a great place to find your paper and decorative items, depending on the store's selection. Arts and crafts stores — as well as scrapbooking stores — can also offer a variety of decorative papers (which you can buy in packs or by the sheet), precut embellishments, and full kits to make your paper engineering look professional in the blink of an eye.

One thing unique to arts-and-crafts-store shopping is the plethora of decorative adornments. This is where you can get really creative with a variety of mediums: paint, textiles, wood, metal, floral craft, and so on. You can add a lot to a simple pop-up card with the addition of a bit of glitter or perhaps some googly eyes to go on a character model.

Hit the sale bins and other doodads at the ends of the aisles and at the register. Often, you can find random stuff that wouldn't normally catch your eye on the shelf.

Making your shopping wallet-friendly: Thrifty sources for new goods

Often, the options before you in arts and crafts stores can be so overwhelming that you just want to curl up in the yarn aisle and take a nap. Sometimes the prices don't help ease the pain, either. Paper engineering can be a fun new hobby, but it can get expensive if you buy a lot of specialty papers.

Try hitting the following places to get the best deals on card, paper, and decorations:

- ✔ **Stationery shop:** Get good-quality paper for less money than the arts and crafts stores charge.
- ✔ **Local print shop:** You can find all the standard paper and card, usually in packs. Paper is much less pricey from the printer than from the stationery shop.
- ✔ **Gift shop:** Some wrapping papers have fabulous patterns printed on them, and they're relatively cheap. If the paper is too thin, bond it to some thin card using a spray-on adhesive, such as Spray Mount. *Warning:* Always use spray-on adhesives in a well ventilated area.
- ✔ **Dollar stores:** In the land of cheapie wonders, you can often find odds and ends, embellishments, wrapping paper, and maybe even some tools for next to nothing in price.
- ✔ **Large discount stores:** You can find good prices and decent sales at the big discount stores. Especially keep your eye open after holidays (when all the wrapping paper goes on sale) and during the back-to-school sales (when art supplies are on sale).
- ✔ **Reuse and/or teacher supply facilities:** The best way to locate this sort of place is to ask your local elementary school or art teacher.

Using the Internet

The Internet is a wonderful place to find paper-engineering materials of all sorts. If you're just starting off, you can have a lot of fun going through craft store Web sites and ordering all sorts of knickknacks. Just go to any search engine and type in "paper engineering supplies." You may be amazed at the number of resources available.

Ordering online works best when you have a lot to order (or when you need specialty items). Small orders can be expensive because of the shipping costs.

Going Green: Recycling and Reusing Materials

Today, more and more people are concerned about doing what they can to preserve the environment. If you're one of those people, Mother Nature thanks you. If you've never really thought about it, even as one individual, you can do your part.

Paper mills clearcut massive quantities of old tree growth every day while glaciers melt, climates and weather patterns shift, and global warming moves in. Not only is global warming bad for Costa Rican frog populations, but it's bad for paper engineers, too. With all that hot, humid air, who knows what kinds of curling and buckling dangers your paper projects are facing! It's a vicious cycle.

So what can you do to be more green (and cut some of your expenses to boot)? Keep the following tips in mind:

- ✔ **Reduce waste.** For you as a paper engineer, this tip means being conscious about using your scrap materials instead of throwing away the excess.

- ✔ **Reuse materials.** Use materials that originally functioned as something else. For example, you can reuse old greeting cards by cutting them into gift tags.

- ✔ **Buy recycled paper.** Look for the recycled logo on paper packs. (*Note:* Although using recycled paper saves trees, the emissions released in the process are still harmful, so reusing is better for the environment.)

So are you ready to go green with your paper-engineering projects? If so, check out this section for where to look for materials, how to reuse paper products, and a fun example project you may want to try.

Locating good, reusable finds

Finding green items is becoming easier as more people become aware of their impact on the environment. Whether you live in a large metropolitan area or in a rural area, you can find reusable materials, supplies, and tools. Here are a few suggestions:

- ✔ **Reuse facilities:** They're cropping up in larger cities, with an audience of artists, teachers, and DIY-ers conscious about reuse. These facilities take in donations of scrap and leftover materials from local businesses and sometimes the public at large. Prices are often subject to the whim of the person working, but they're almost always dirt cheap.

- ✔ **Yard and garage sales:** You can find all sorts of fun materials that other people have bought but never got around to using. This is your chance to pick up a real bargain!

- ✔ **Thrift stores and secondhand stores:** These places can yield great finds. Don't be afraid to tell employees what you're looking for. They may have just the right thing hidden away in the back room.

- ✔ **Friends, neighbors, and other craftsters:** Communicate with others about your new hobby. You can bring a wealth of someone else's trash to your workstation.

Of course, there's no need to run out to buy something to reuse. Every day you use items around your home that you can reuse for your paper-engineering projects. Just look around, and you'll be surprised at what you find. Here's what I like to reuse:

- **Magazines:** These make great montages (see Chapter 5) and backgrounds.

- **Greeting cards:** These are a good source of pictures that you can cut out for your projects.

- **Cereal boxes:** Use cereal boxes for a prototype model of a new trial design.

Keep your saved materials in a special place so they don't get pitched. I'm a hoarder. I always like to keep things that may come in useful someday. My wife, on the other hand, loves to clear out. We're in a constant tension between keep and throw away. I have little hiding places around the house where I keep useful stuff so that it doesn't get thrown out.

Recycling paper

If you're a crafty, hands-on type of person, you may want to experiment and make your own paper. Doing so isn't that difficult if you have a little patience, some basic raw materials, and some free time one afternoon or evening. One caveat: The homemade paper I explain how to make in this section isn't strong enough to make paper-engineering mechanisms like those in most of the projects in this book. However, it's great for decorations or for making paper-based art projects with your family.

Project 2-1: Homemade Paper

The essential ingredient of paper is fiber. When I was young, my family and I had a go at making paper from nettle plants. We had to boil the nettle stalks in caustic soda to break down the fibers and then sieve them out to make the paper. We only did it once — even after all these years I can still remember the revolting smell! But even today, I've had fun making recycled paper with my own children.

Follow these simple steps to make your own homemade paper from recycled materials. Newsprint works well, but try to use paper with no ink on it.

Tools and Materials

Paper to recycle (about 20 letter-size sheets)	Water
1-cup measuring cup	Large plastic bowl, bigger than the wooden frame
Wooden frame, slightly larger than the paper you're making	Decorative elements, such as dried flowers, pieces of colored thread, or glitter
Fine mesh screen, slightly larger than the wooden frame (plain weave curtain netting is perfect)	2 sheets of felt, larger than the wooden frame
Stapler	Rolling pin
Blender	

1. **Rip up the paper into 1" squares.**

   Tear up enough paper to fill a 1-cup measuring cup.

2. **Staple the mesh screen to the frame (see Figure 2-3).**

   Keep the screen tight and flat, just like you want your paper to be.

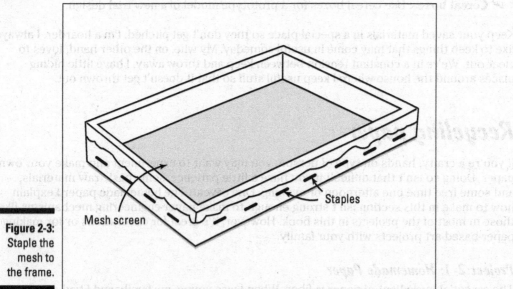

Staples

Mesh screen

Figure 2-3:
Staple the
mesh to
the frame.

3. **Shred the paper in your blender.**

   First make sure you cleaned your blender after your recent milkshake. Half-fill your blender with water and add some paper squares; blend the paper until the water looks like thin oatmeal. Tip the result into your plastic bowl. Repeat until all your paper is pulped.

4. **Add some extras to the mix.**

   To make your paper interesting, add some little extras — short lengths of colored thread, some glitter, or perhaps some small flower heads. Refer to Figure 2-4 to see how extras can jazz up some paper. Stir it all in.

   When making paper, don't blend your extras! The blades from the blender chop the interesting bits into fine particles and spoil the effect.

5. **Sieve out some pulp onto your mesh frame.**

   Give the pulp a good stir; then scoop out some of the mix with the mesh frame. As you do, the water runs straight through the mesh, leaving a layer of pulp that will become your paper.

6. **Flip the pulp out onto a sheet of felt.**

   Place a sheet of felt on your work surface. Turn the mesh so that the pulp falls onto the felt in one flat piece. This process is called *couching*.

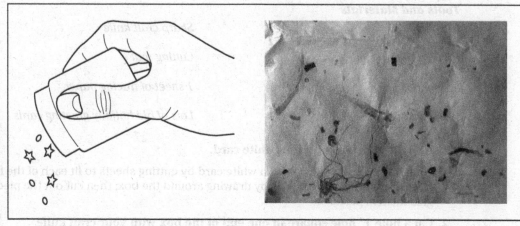

Figure 2-4:
Add some
extras
into your
paper mix.

7. Cover the felt and squeeze out the water.

Cover the felt and layer of pulp with another piece of felt. Roll the water out with a rolling pin, pressing down firmly as you do so. Roll from one edge, across the felt, to the other edge.

8. Dry the paper to complete the process.

Leave the paper between the felt and let it dry overnight.

Never tip your waste fiber down a domestic sink. The waste can congeal and block your drain. Instead, put the waste into a sturdy plastic garbage bag and put it in the trash.

Feel free to experiment with making homemade paper. Try using different amounts of paper in the pulp for different thicknesses of paper. Add different extras in Step 4. Making paper yourself can be very satisfying. The results often look great, and it's good for the environment.

A green Christmas: Making a winter scene from reused holiday cards

At the end of the holiday season, my family collects all our cards. I always wonder what I should do with them. All that quality printing and beautiful artwork — it's a shame to see it go to waste. So here's a fun project to do in the winter evenings before spring arrives.

Project 2-2: Winter Peephole Box

This project is to make a 3D scene by reusing cards. Look through the hole in the end of the box, and you see a whole 3D vista laid out before you.

Tools and Materials

Old shoebox   Sharp craft knife

6 sheets of thin white card   Cutting mat

Scissors   1 sheet of tracing paper

White school glue   Lots of old holiday greeting cards

1. **Line the shoebox with thin white card.**

   Line the inside of your box with white card by cutting sheets to fit each of the five inner faces. Measure out the pieces by drawing around the box; then cut out the pieces and glue them in place.

2. **Cut a hole 1″ hole square in one end of the box with your craft knife (see Figure 2-5).**

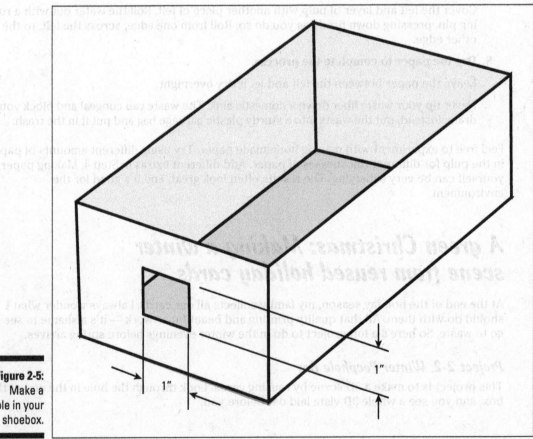

Figure 2-5:
Make a
hole in your
shoebox.

1″

1″

3. **Add a skylight to the lid.**

The lid lets the light in while blocking out distractions. To make the lid, just follow these steps:

1. Cut a hole in the lid using the craft knife. The hole need to be 1" smaller than the lid (see Figure 2-6).

2. Cut your tracing paper so that it fits inside the lid.

3. Glue it into place on the inside of the lid.

4. **Sort your greeting cards by the size of the images.**

Sort the cards so that small-scale things are at one end of your heap of cards and large-scale things are at the other.

5. **Choose your images and cut out the pieces.**

Just as in real life, things that are far away need to appear smaller than closer objects. Go through your cards and choose which pictures you're going to use. Perhaps choose some large festive-looking people for the foreground, some medium-sized buildings for the middle, and some small hills and trees for the background.

6. **Make a stand for each character in your model.**

Cut out triangle shapes from card so you can glue a stand to each character (like the one in Figure 2-7) .

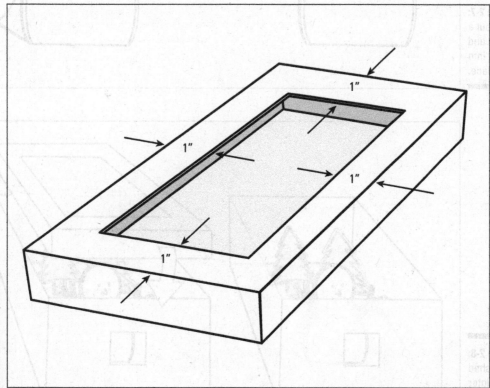

Figure 2-6:
Create a
tracing
paper
skylight
in the lid.

7. **Arrange each character inside the box.**

   Before you glue everything down, check through the peephole to make sure the scene looks good.

8. **After you're happy with their placement, glue the characters down and let the glue dry.**

   Your project is done. Put the lid on the box and shine a light on the tracing paper. Look through the peephole to see a wonderful winter scene. See Figure 2-8.

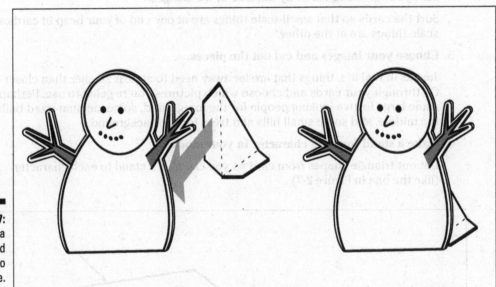

Figure 2-7:
Cut out a stand and stick it into place.

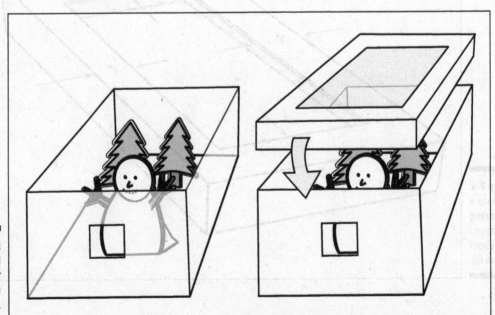

Figure 2-8:
The finished Winter Peephole Box.

Chapter 3

Making Your Paper-Engineering Workshop Work for You

In This Chapter
▶ Setting up your workshop
▶ Stocking your workshop with tools and materials
▶ Using your computer

*W*hen making your paper-engineering and pop-up projects, your workspace is your lair, your haven, your safe place. It's the place where you can think up ideas and craft them to fruition. But just because you're playing inventor doesn't mean you have to hide away in your secret underground lab, toiling away by torchlight. Engineers usually prefer to work in well-lit, semiorganized areas, with all the necessary tools within reach.

To make all those beautiful creations, you need a workspace that meets your needs. This chapter explains how to set up your beginning workspace, what tools and materials to include, and how to keep everything clean and easily accessible.

Creating Space for Your Workspace

You can try designing and making your paper models on the floor on a newspaper or spread over your knee in front of the TV, but these conditions aren't really ideal. If you want to take your paper engineering seriously, you need to think seriously about where you work. Having a space designated for your paper engineering — where you store your tools, have ample room to work, and can easily find everything you need — is key. Setting up a work area needn't be expensive or difficult; it just needs a little planning. This section gives you the lowdown on making room and on keeping the area clean and organized.

Setting out your workspace

You may be lucky enough to have a permanent workspace. Even a small area where you need to pack everything away when you've finished your paper-engineering projects is better than not having a designated work area at all. No matter what type of space you have, the basics of your workspace are the same: You need light, a chair, and a work surface.

Lighting: See what I'm saying?

By selecting the right lighting, you can avoid the eyestrain and headaches that come from working in poor lighting conditions, get your colors right, and make sure all those sharp blades are cutting the things you really intend to cut.

The ideal workspace is in front of a large window, with shaded daylight streaming in to evenly illuminate your desk without being too bright. Unfortunately, you may not be that lucky. In fact, my workroom is in a box room at the back of the house with a tiny window and only limited light. The lack of natural light means that I need to think about lighting very carefully.

You may get good lighting from your room's overhead light, but in most cases, the room light is behind you in the center of the room, so your body casts a shadow over your desk. For perfect lighting, you really do need a desk light. The ideal desk light has a wide reflector to make the light soft and diffuse and should be adjustable for height and position.

For the best working environment, you need bright but diffuse lighting, such as from a clear light that doesn't cast harsh shadows. Consider the following types of bulbs for your workspace:

- ✔ **Halogen bulbs:** Many desk lights use halogen bulbs. These lamps emit a clean, bright light, but they do have a couple of disadvantages. They're harsh, and they run really hot. You can overcome the harsh lighting problem by having two or more lights or by reflecting the light off a white surface such as a wall or ceiling. However, the heat may still be a problem.

   If you use a halogen light, don't touch the bulb or the casing around the bulb. Keep your paper and other flammable materials a safe distance away, too.

- ✔ **Energy-saving fluorescent bulbs:** I've recently changed to using these bulbs. They have a less harsh light than the halogen bulbs, run cold, and are kind to the planet, too. Perfect! Well, nearly. The light from these bulbs isn't a natural daylight color, so choosing color schemes can be difficult.

- ✔ **White light LEDs (light-emitting diodes):** These lights run cool, are very efficient electrically, and look fantastic. However, the light from white LEDs tends to be very blue, which makes them not-so-good for working on colors. LED lights are more expensive, too.

- ✔ **Incandescent bulbs:** These standard light bulbs are cheap and easily available. They're not very efficient, so they use more electricity than other types. The light they give off is a bit on the orange side, but overall they make for a good desk light.

When you're working on colors, try to use daylight as your light source. If this isn't possible, then halogen or normal incandescent light bulbs are you best choice.

Your chair

In your workspace, you spend the majority of your time in your chair. Although a chair that helps you maintain good posture may be pricey, it's a good investment. Hunching over your workspace can put a real strain on your neck and back.

The only person who can choose your chair is you. Keep the following tips in mind during your search:

✔ Visit your local office supplier and try out all the chairs in the store, even the expensive ones.

✔ Make sure you get a chair with height adjustment and a proper back support. When seated with your feet flat on the floor, your upper legs should be level with the floor. (See Figure 3-1 for a complete visual of the ideal chair fitting.) *Note:* You may need to use a footrest to obtain this position.

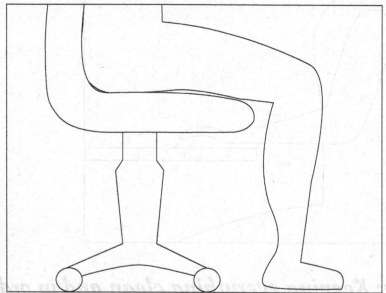

Figure 3-1:
Make sure your chair is the correct height.

If you buy a chair with casters and your work area is carpeted, get a plastic mat to keep beneath your chair so you can keep on rolling with ease.

Your work surface

Your work surface, most likely a desk or table, is the space where you actually make your paper-engineering creations. Like your chair, your work surface's height can affect your posture. If it's too low, you have to bend down and put strain on your back. If it's too high, you sit with raised shoulders and put strain on your shoulders and neck. Therefore, finding a surface of the appropriate height is essential. So what's the appropriate height? When sitting at your table with your shoulders relaxed, your forearms should rest level on the tabletop as Figure 3-2 shows.

In addition to the work surface's height, keep the following points in mind:

✔ **Size:** You want a good-sized table where you can spread out and easily work without everything piling up.

If you can swing it, get a desk long enough so you can have a work area and a storage area, as well as a place for your computer. This extra room makes your life so much easier.

✔ **Surface:** Look for a table or desk with a smooth and hard-wearing surface. A smooth surface is easy to keep clean, and a hard-wearing surface doesn't dent if your scissors slip.

✔ **Sturdiness:** Make sure the table or desk is sturdy. A wobbly table is no fun to work with, especially when you're cutting with a knife.

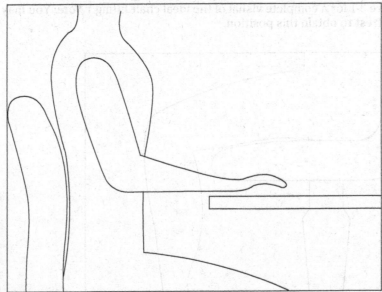

Figure 3-2:
The work surface is at about elbow level.

Storage: Keeping everything clean and in order

Although my wife may laugh at my saying this next bit, keeping your work area neat and tidy is very important. Not only does keeping everything arranged increase your efficiency, but it also makes your work area safer, so try to keep things tidy while you work instead of cleaning up a whole mess at the end.

My own workspace may not be clinically neat, but I *do* try to be tidy, I really do! Still, I like to think that a bit of ordered chaos is a sign of a creative mind (even though my wife says it's just a mess). Just make sure that any disorganization is intended to encourage creativity and keep the items you need close by, not to give those scissors, compass points, and craft knives a chance to bury themselves in a stack of papers.

Whether you have a permanent work area or are working at the kitchen table, storage is vital. After all, if you're going to put things away as you finish using them, you need to know where they go. This section points out some ways to store your tools and materials while maintaining easy access.

Mother knows best: Putting your tools in their places

When starting out doing paper engineering, you may not have tons of tools, but you still need to keep them organized and out of the way when you're not using them. Consider the two storage methods I use:

✔ **Small plastic container with dividers:** I use one to hold my most commonly used tools. Mine contains my favorite scissors, a sharp knife, a selection of pens and pencils, and some tweezers. This is the container that sits at my side as I work, kind of like a loyal dog. Young students often have these containers to hold their pencils, scissors, and such.

✔ **Toolbox:** A toolbox or tackle box is a great way to keep your tools safe and to make them accessible. It need not be expensive, just something that can house your many tools in any orderly fashion. I use a plastic toolbox, shown in Figure 3-3, that I bought from a local hardware store. I use this to keep pens, scissors, brushes, and other bits and pieces in. I like the type that opens out to reveal several trays. These trays let you keep all your different tools separate and organized.

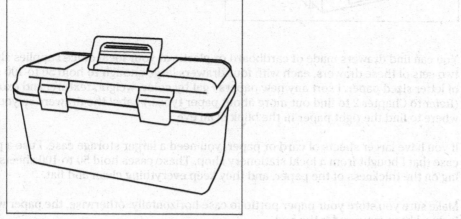

Figure 3-3:
A simple plastic toolbox.

Keeping your card and paper straight

One of the best ways to keep your workspace in order as you work is to use a small plastic container on your desk. There, you can deposit all your scrap paper *(offcut)* as you create it instead of having it litter your workspace. You can also immediately throw away the smaller pieces that aren't worth reusing.

As for your commonly used paper (such as photocopier paper and 230-micron pulp board, my workhorse card), put a few open-top cardboard boxes on your desk where you can easily access them. If you work in an office, you probably have access to the lids from packs of photocopier paper, which make perfect trays to store your everyday paper.

Of course, you need somewhere to store the materials that don't fit on your desk, too. And purchasing and collecting supplies can be addictive! You start off buying just some thin paper, and then you quickly move onto the sweet stuff, colored paper. Next thing you know, you're adding to your collection with a few sheets of nice homemade paper. While out in town, you see some nice textured paper and buy a pack or two. Before you know it, you have a mountain of different papers and you can't even find the one you want. It's time to sort out your problem, and a good paper storage system is the solution.

One of my favorite storage units is a set of drawers made from corrugated cardboard (refer to Figure 3-4). A set of drawers like this is inexpensive and easy to move. It keeps your paper flat so that it doesn't curl, and the drawers protect any colored papers from fading in the sunlight.

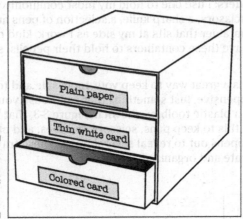

Figure 3-4:
A cardboard chest of drawers.

Plain paper

Thin white card

Colored card

You can find drawers made of cardboard or plastic at your local office supplies shop. I have two sets of these drawers, each with four drawers large enough to hold 50 to 100 sheets of letter-sized paper. I sort any new papers I get by color, weight, texture, and exoticness. (Refer to Chapter 2 to find out more about paper types.) Label the drawers so you know where to find the right paper in the blink of an eye.

If you have larger sheets of card or paper, you need a larger storage case. I use a portfolio case that I bought from a local stationery shop. These cases hold 50 to 100 sheets, depending on the thickness of the paper, and they keep everything clean and flat.

Make sure you store your paper portfolio case horizontally; otherwise, the paper will bend inside. I keep mine under the bed.

Tools of the Trade: What Your Workshop Needs

You may not need heavy machinery, and you don't need to plug in paper-engineering tools, but they're just as vital to the job as a circular saw or a power planer is to a woodworker. With the basic tools in this section, you can get started and successfully create any project in this book.

Scissors: Your most important tool

I bet you thought you'd rarely use scissors after you got out of elementary school. Well, I hope you paid attention then, because you use those cutting skills a lot with paper engineering. Of all the tools, you use scissors the most.

Scissors come in all sizes and shapes. I have several pairs of scissors for paper engineering, but here are my favorites (see Figure 3-5):

✔ A pair that I use just for scoring

✔ A 3" pair for general cutting

✔ A super sharp pair with 2" blades for intricate work

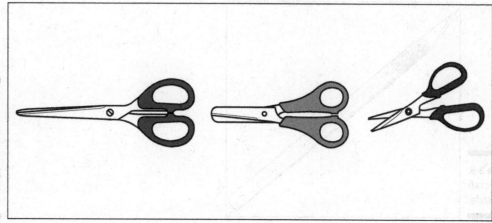

Figure 3-5:
Scoring
scissors,
general
scissors,
and super
fine
scissors.

Because you use your scissors so much, it really is worth spending the time and money to get the right ones for you. Look for scissors with a nice, easy action, and make sure they cut well. Scissors are tools you want to try before you buy, so if possible, don't buy them online; a good art supply or stationery shop should be willing to let you test them out. You can't tell whether scissors are good for you if they're in plastic wrap. Take a few pieces of paper and card to the store with you and look for the following traits:

- ✔ The pair should cut cleanly and with as little effort as possible. Make sure the scissors open and close freely but don't feel loose.

  Don't buy scissors that are too stiff. Your hands will tire quickly if you have lots of cutting to do.

- ✔ The two blades should be just touching over the full length of the cut.

- ✔ Look for a blade length of about 3". Longer blades are difficult to control accurately, and shorter blades are harder to use neatly.

The sharp craft knife: Your cutting edge

At first you may not be comfortable cutting paper with a sharp craft knife instead of your trusty scissors, but craft knives are useful in paper engineering. Although scissors are great for cutting around the outside of shapes, you really need a knife to cut holes in the paper or do fine detail work.

The best type of knife to use is the X-Acto style craft knife or craft-based scalpel (see Figure 3-6). These knives use disposable blades that are easy to obtain from your craft shop. I use No. 11 blades on a scalpel handle.

Make sure you always have extra blades for your craft knife on hand. It's surprising how quickly paper and card blunt the edges of your blades.

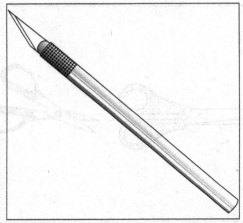

Figure 3-6:
A craft
knife.

Cutting mat: Protect your assets!

You need only one slip with your scoring scissors or your craft knife to ruin your best kitchen table or desk and make your significant other a tad peeved. To avoid slips, invest in a good quality cutting mat. A *self-healing cutting mat* is basically a large mat made from two layers of a special plastic. The top layer is soft and gives under your blade. The bottom layer is rigid and protects your work surface. Using a cutting mat keeps your blades sharp, protects your work surface, and keeps you from getting in trouble.

Through the advancement of science, you can run your super-sharp craft knife over the mat and not even leave any cut marks in the mat — hence the term *self-healing*. I have two mats: one small, letter-size mat (8.5" x 11") and one larger A3-size mat (11.7" x 16.5"). To find a cutting mat that's right for you, just look at the ones available in your local craft store. If you're just starting out, I recommend the letter-size mat.

Your cutting mat doesn't like heat, so when you're not using it, don't lean it against a radiator or heating vent. Also, your cutting mat isn't a coaster, so don't set your mug of coffee on it. When you aren't using it, find somewhere you can keep it stored level and flat so that it doesn't kink or curl.

Tools for measuring and moving paper

As you get more adept in your paper engineering, you may want to add some other basic tools to help you with the fine details:

✔ **Ruler:** Although the ruler is one of your most important pieces of equipment, it doesn't need to cost a fortune. Some paper engineers use expensive aluminum or steel rulers, but I prefer the clear, cheap plastic variety. They're usually very accurate, and you can see through them, which is useful when marking or measuring.

✔ **Tweezers:** Tweezers are great for those fiddly jobs when you need to hold two pieces of paper together. For example, when you're gluing two pieces of paper, you can get the glue to set quickly by pinching the two parts together. Often you can just grip the pieces between your finger and thumb, but when that's not possible, tweezers come in handy.

Some tweezers have a ridged surface inside their ends, which can leave marks in the paper. Your best bet is to use tweezers with smooth inner surfaces. The local drugstore is a good place to buy tweezers.

✔ **Chopsticks:** No, you don't need chopsticks in your toolbox in case you get hungry at 10 p.m. and want to order out Chinese. Chopsticks are great as an extra long finger. For example, if you're making a thin paper tube and need to glue the edges together, you can use a chopstick when you're trying to put some parts of paper together but you can't get your fingers in to hold everything together.

✔ **Drawing compass:** You need a compass for measuring and drawing circles. Compasses come in a whole range of types. You can pay an awful lot for a top-of-the-line compass; luckily, a cheap one works fine. Look for a compass and pencil in a school geometry set.

✔ **Protractor:** You may occasionally need a protractor for measuring angles. You can get a protractor in a school geometry set along with your compass; otherwise, check the shelves in your local stationery store with the rulers.

✔ **Calipers:** Calipers, which allow you to measure paper thickness, are a very valuable addition to a paper engineer's toolbox (check out Figure 3-7). Most paper engineering tools are relatively cheap, but a good pair of calipers can be quite pricey. Ask for some calipers for your birthday. You can find calipers in most hardware stores and tool depots. See Chapter 2 for more on paper thickness.

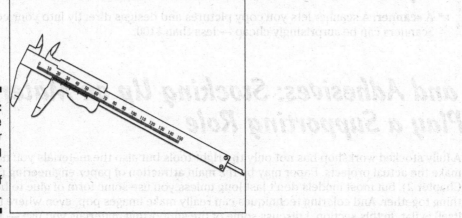

Figure 3-7:
You use calipers for measuring the thickness of paper.

Including computer hardware in your space

A computer can make your life a lot easier when you're designing and refining paper-engineering and pop-up projects. With a computer, you can quickly and easily change your designs, reprint, and construct your prototypes as many times as you need without the work that'd be involved if you were to do everything manually. You can also easily add color to your designs on the computer and then print them out on an inkjet printer. And you can even go online to look at other people's projects and get some design inspiration.

You don't need to go out and spend thousands of dollars. You may already have most of the basic pieces of hardware that are useful for paper engineering. Even if you don't, you may be able to buy them used. (Check with your friends and family to see whether they're selling any of this equipment. You can also check out www.craigslist.com or www.ebay.com for good bargains.)

So what hardware do you need? Look into adding these items to your workspace:

- ✔ **A computer:** Whether you use a Mac or a PC, you want a fairly up-to-date machine. It doesn't need to be top-of-the-line, but you do need something that can run modern programs without breaking into too much of a sweat. Aim for a processor running faster than 1 gigahertz (GHz) and at least 1 gigabyte (GB) of RAM.

- ✔ **A printer:** You want a printer that handles card. Surprisingly, many cheap color inkjet printers are excellent for printing onto card. I use a simple $100 Epson printer that I've had for a couple of years now.

  When searching for a printer, check out the printer manufacturer's Web site for information about whether you can print onto card before you buy.

- ✔ **A scanner:** A scanner lets you copy pictures and designs directly into your computer. Scanners can be surprisingly cheap — less than $100.

Color and Adhesives: Stocking Up on Materials That Play a Supporting Role

A fully stocked workshop has not only the right tools but also the materials you need to make the actual projects. Paper may be the main attraction of paper engineering (see Chapter 2), but most models don't last long unless you use some form of glue to hold everything together. And coloring techniques can really make images pop, even where the paper itself is flat. In this section, I discuss some of the supporting materials you use — and use up — in paper engineering.

Using the right glue for the job

Visit any craft and hobby shop, and you see shelves groaning under a bewildering selection of glues. You can find different glues for every occasion. Fortunately, for the paper and card projects in this book, you need only three main types of glue (see Figure 3-8).

Figure 3-8:
Different
types of
glue.

The following list gives you a rundown of the three types of glue:

- **White school glue:** White school glue — or PVA (polyvinyl acetate) — is the glue you use most often in the projects in this book. It's water-soluble, meaning that it dissolves in water and doesn't give off any unpleasant fumes. It works by soaking into the surface of the paper. Because of this, it doesn't work on shiny or waterproof materials.

   White school glue takes a little while to dry, which can be upsetting if you're seeking instant gratification for your efforts. However, for the perfectionist, this wait time allows you to rearrange and correct any small mistakes you've made. You need to spread the glue thin so the paper doesn't wrinkle.

- **Glue sticks:** Unlike white school glue, glue sticks have very little water in them, so they don't cause the paper to wrinkle. They also dry very quickly.

- **Solvent-based glue:** You use solvent-based glues to affix materials that have a water-proof surface. This is the job that your tried-and-true white school glue just can't handle. Keep a small tube of solvent-based glue in your paper-engineering toolbox for when you're decorating a greeting card with a few sequins or adding some googly eyes to a character.

Adding elements of color

When I design paper models, I usually make the model from plain white card. After I'm happy with the model, I add color. What a difference it makes! A model that looked good in white paper suddenly looks fantastic. You want to make sure you have the capabilities to add color to your designs. This section looks at a few materials to include in your workspace.

Crayons, pencils, and pens: Not just for kids

One of the easiest ways to incorporate colors in your design is to buy crayons and pens for your workspace. By having a decent assortment of colors at your disposal, you can make a dull piece of paper come to life. Here's how you can use these coloring tools:

- ✔ **Crayons:** Not only do crayons come in a huge range of rich colors, but they're generally pretty affordable. Pick up a pack of 24 or 36 crayons for just a few dollars at the local stationery shop or large discount store.

- ✔ **Colored pencils:** These work best for subtle shading effects and for drawing fine details, complementing the artwork of your crayons and felt-tipped pens. Colored pencils don't provide as rich of a color as crayons, and they're not good for coloring large areas.

- ✔ **Water-based felt-tipped pens (markers):** They're cheap and easy to get hold of, and they make rich, deep colors. The problem with these pens is that the water gets into the card and can make the surface uneven. If you choose to use water-based felt-tipped pens, be careful not to saturate the paper.

  Another problem with this type of pen is that the colors can run. If you draw a light-colored pen over a dark color, the dark color is sponged into the point of the felt pen. When you use the pen again, it smudges with the darker color. What a way to ruin a project!

- ✔ **Solvent-based felt-tipped pens:** The colors from these pens are rich and vibrant, and they don't smudge in the same way that the watercolor pens do. However, they're much more expensive than the water-based variety.

  Use solvent-based pens in a well-ventilated area. Keep the windows and doors open so you can breathe free and stay conscious.

Coloring your world with paper

When assembling your workspace, you want to gather a wide assortment of papers. One great way to add color to your designs is to use paper with different colors and patterns. You can save time and effort by treating yourself to the myriad of colored and patterned papers already available to you. Just mixing patterns and solid colors can have a wonderful effect when you do it with a keen eye for design. Check out your local stationery store, arts and crafts store, or printer to wade through the large numbers of different colors and patterns. Chapter 2 gives you an overview of the different types of paper available.

You can also create your own colored paper using the following paints and inks (see Chapter 4 for coloring techniques):

- ✔ **Watercolor paint:** These paints are sold in either tubes or blocks of solid color. Creating washes with watercolor paint is a simple but effective technique. Watercolor paint gives you a slightly uneven, mottled color.

- ✔ **Marbling ink:** Using marbling inks from your local craft store, you can create paper that has swirls and veins in it so it really does look like marble.

Chapter 4

Putting Everything Together: Techniques and Safety Tips

In This Chapter

▶ Using templates and marking your card

▶ Cutting and folding

▶ Applying glue

▶ Coloring paper

*O*ne of my first adventures in paper engineering was making an elephant mask from the back of a cereal box. There was a picture of a child on the box, happily raising his elephant mask trunk with the simple pull of a tab. It was inspiring. I hurriedly cut out the pieces, glued them together, and tried on my elephant mask. But when I pulled the tab, nothing happened. I tried again, and to my utter disappointment, the trunk stayed put. When I looked closer after taking the mask off, I realized that not only had I glued the tab to the mask itself but I'd also gotten a mess of glue stains in all sorts of the wrong places, including my own hair!

Although you've probably been using scissors and glue for as long as you can remember, you can discover some handy techniques, as well as some important safety pointers, in this chapter. These tips can help you to make your project as good as it can be while also keeping you (and your hair) clean and safe. After all, nothing's sadder than an elephant mask with a droopy trunk.

Measuring and Marking Your Paper

Engineers are all about planning. And for paper engineers, that planning means carefully measuring and marking the paper or card. Whether you're doing a project from this book or creating your own design, you need to show yourself where to cut, where to score and fold, and where to apply glue. A little planning can mean the difference between a crooked construction and an architectural masterpiece.

For most of the projects in this book, I provide a template at the beginning of the project (see Figure 4-1 for a sample). A *template* is essentially a pattern, not necessarily full-size, that you can copy on your paper or card to create your project. It can sometimes look like some sort of extraterrestrial subway system, but don't let yourself get alienated — I have the key for you.

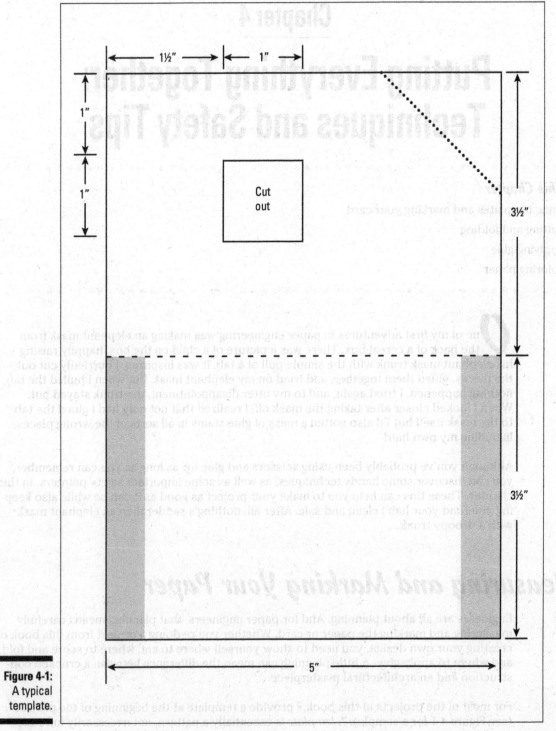

Figure 4-1:
A typical
template.

As you can see, this template has a variety of line types and some shaded areas. For clarity, I use the same lines throughout the book — and you may want to use this same system when you mark your own card. Here's a brief rundown of what all this stuff means:

- ✔ **Dotted lines:** Lines with a series of small dots show where to score to make *valley folds* (see Figure 4-2). These folds form the letter *v*, making a small valley in the card. You need to score along dotted lines before you cut out the card. (To understand scoring, check out the "Scoring for crisp folds" section later in this chapter.)

- ✔ **Dashed lines:** Lines made up of small dashes show where to score to make hill folds (refer to Figure 4-2). In a *hill fold*, sometimes referred to as a *mountain fold*, you fold the paper or card downward to make a little hill shape.

- ✔ **Solid lines:** These lines show where to cut. You usually use scissors for the cutting. Occasionally, the solid line appears inside a shape, sometimes with the words *Cut Out* also located inside the shape. In this case, you need to use a sharp craft knife to cut the solid line. (Check out the "Keen cutting" section for more information.)

- ✔ **Gray area:** These areas show you where to glue. Not getting glue outside these areas is important. Otherwise, all the wrong pieces can end up stuck together.

When marking your card for paper engineering, measuring is one of the most important techniques you need to master. Measuring helps you make sure everything fits together properly. Without accurate measurement, making mechanisms that work well is difficult. This section shows you how to measure and copy your templates using a ruler, drawing compass, and protractor.

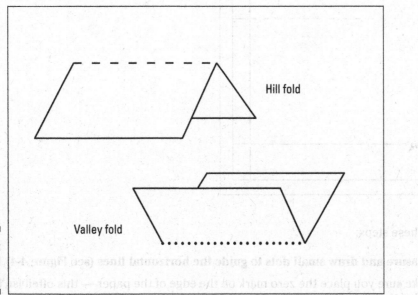

Figure 4-2:
Hill and
valley folds.

Measuring up: The ruler

In paper engineering, you do almost all your measuring with a ruler. Although the ruler is one of the most important pieces of equipment in your paper engineer's toolbox, it doesn't need to cost a fortune. Some paper engineers use expensive aluminum or steel rulers, but I prefer the cheap plastic variety. They're usually very accurate, and because they're plastic, you can see through them, which is often useful when marking or measuring. I say go splurge a few cents at the corner shop and start measuring up!

To mark your paper, you need a ruler (preferably clear plastic), a pencil, and an eraser. The following steps explain how to copy a template onto a piece of paper. Check out the template in Figure 4-3 ready to be copied.

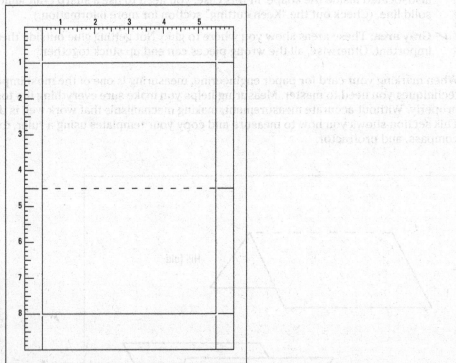

Figure 4-3:
Create this
simple
template.

Follow these steps:

1. **Measure and draw small dots to guide the horizontal lines (see Figure 4-4).**

Make sure you place the zero mark on the edge of the paper — this often isn't the very end of the ruler. Draw small dots next to the appropriate marks on the ruler, as close to the edge of the page as possible. Using the smallest dot that you can still clearly see — the smaller the dot, the less room for error. On the other edge of the card, make the same marks again.

2. Line up the ruler with a pair of dots.

The ruler's edge just touches the edge of the first two dots; spend a little time making sure you do this as accurately as possible. Press down firmly on the ruler so it doesn't move.

3. Draw a line connecting the dots.

Use your pencil to lightly draw a line that goes between the two dots and extends past them. Make sure your ruler doesn't move while you're drawing the line.

You don't need to be super accurate to draw a dotted or dashed line to indicate where to score the paper. Press down hard on the ruler so that it doesn't move and then draw dashes. Dots are kind of hard to draw with a pencil, so just use short dashes.

4. Repeat this process with two vertical lines (see Figure 4-5).

This basic process is the same with all the templates in this book. Copy the templates carefully and accurately for the best results.

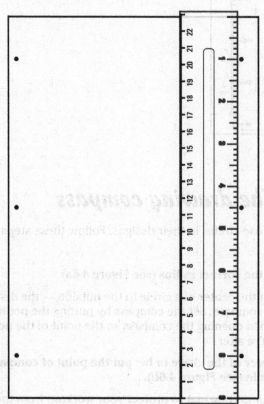

Figure 4-4:
Measuring for the horizontal lines.

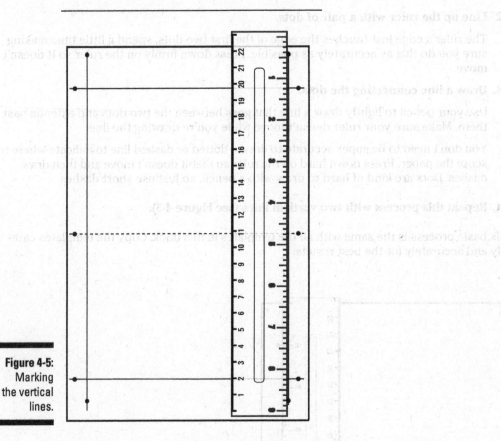

Figure 4-5:
Marking
the vertical
lines.

Doing the rounds: The drawing compass

Some of the templates in this book use circles in their designs. Follow these steps to accurately draw a circle:

1. **Set your drawing compass to the correct radius (see Figure 4-6a).**

   The *radius* is the distance from the center of a circle to the outside — the distance between the two ends of your compass. Set the compass by putting the point on the zero mark on your ruler and then opening the compass so the point of the pencil touches the measurement you're after.

2. **Mark where you want the center of the circle to be; put the point of compass on the center mark and draw the circle (see Figure 4-6b).**

   Put your piece of paper on your cutting mat to protect your worktop from the compass point. Hold the hinge of the compass as you draw the circle to make sure the radius doesn't change.

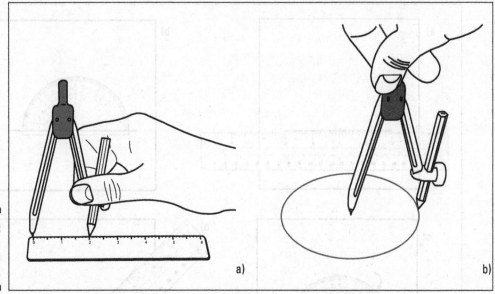

Figure 4-6:
Drawing a
circle with a
compass.

a)

b)

Getting a new angle: The protractor

For some paper-engineering projects, you may need to use a protractor to measure accurate angles on your templates. Follow these steps to mark out an angle using a protractor.

1. **Lightly draw the line you're measuring your angle from (refer to Figure 4-7a).**

   The line needs to run a couple of inches past the point where you're measuring the angle.

2. **Line up your protractor with the baseline (see Figure 4-7b).**

   The long baseline on the protractor needs to line up with the baseline you just drew. Line up the center cross on the protractor with where you want the point (vertex) of the angle to be.

3. **Put a pencil dot on your paper at the correct angle (see Figure 4-7c).**

   For example, if you're making a 45° angle, put a small dot next to the number 45.

4. **Use a pencil and ruler to complete the angle (check out Figure 4-7d).**

   Line up the ruler with the point of the angle and the new dot. Then draw in the new angle line.

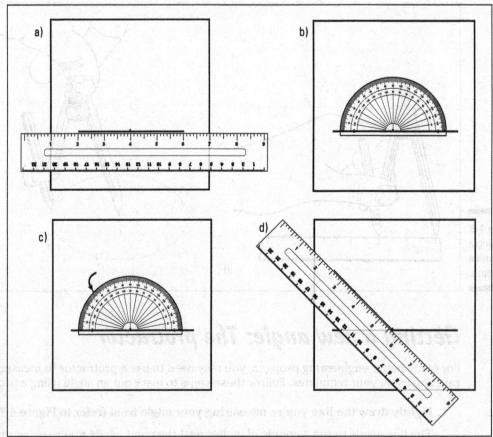

Figure 4-7:
Measuring
angles with
a protractor.

Tracing to a T: Tricks of the Trade

Tracing is an important technique that you may use a lot when you're working from templates or when you're copying from your own notes. Using a ruler to measure and draw straight lines is great when you're copying a simple template, but if you want to copy an intricate design, your trusty ruler may not be up to the task. Unless you have a really good eye, you probably need to trace the pattern that you like onto your piece of paper. Tracing is simple if you follow these basic steps.

Because proper tracing paper is expensive, you can use wax paper (greaseproof paper) instead; it works almost as well and is available from most supermarkets. Buy sheets rather than rolls so that they stay flat on your paper.

You need the following items to trace a pattern:

- The piece you want to trace
- Tracing paper or wax paper
- Masking tape
- A pencil with a soft lead (2B)

✔ An eraser

✔ The paper you want to copy the image onto

Follow these steps to accurately trace your pattern:

1. **Tape the tracing paper over the design you want to trace.**

   Use masking tape if possible; masking tape is easier to remove.

2. **Carefully draw over the design with your pencil.**

   Make sure you keep your pencil sharp for the best quality tracing.

3. **Unstick the tracing paper from the design, flip the tracing paper over, and trace over the design on the back of the sheet.**

   If you don't flip over the image and retrace it in this step, your design will be reversed when you copy it onto your new sheet of paper. If you're going to cut out the image, it's often a good idea to draw a reversed image on the back of the piece of paper you'll be cutting out so you keep the front clean. In that case, you can skip this step.

4. **Flip the tracing paper over and tape it to the paper you're copying onto.**

5. **Using your pencil, scribble over the lines of your design.**

   As you do this, the pencil lead on the back of your tracing paper transfers to the paper you're copying onto.

6. **Remove the tracing paper from your paper.**

   Carefully discard the tracing paper. Be careful that you don't get your hands messy from all the pencil lead on the tracing paper.

Scoring and Cutting Techniques

From folding to cutting, a wealth of paper-engineering pro know-how is right here before your eyes. Although some of these techniques are basic, the room for error in paper engineering isn't huge. You aren't in kindergarten anymore, cutting and gluing construction paper chains; you're now in the big leagues. Follow these simple tips and guidelines to make your paper projects really stand out from the crowd's.

Paper cuts, though not serious, can be very painful. The edges of some types of paper are sharp, like a fine saw. Try to avoid pulling paper along your skin as you cut, fold, and glue your paper.

Scoring for crisp folds

Scoring is simply a technique for putting a dent into a piece of card to make sure that it creases where you want it to, making your folds crisp and sharp. You score the paper after you mark your card but before you cut it out. The dotted lines on the template represent valley fold lines, and dashed lines on the templates are hill fold lines. (See the "Measuring and Marking Your Paper" section earlier in this chapter for more information.)

TIP

Some scissors score well, whereas others just cut through the card. Be careful not to use a very sharp pair. Find a pair that makes a clean dent. Then keep note of which scissors are best for different tasks. Scissors aren't always multipurpose. I have a favorite pair of scissors for cutting and a different pair for scoring.

To make a good score, follow these techniques:

1. **With the paper on your cutting mat, line up your ruler with the dotted or dashed line and press the ruler down firmly.**

   Make sure the ruler lines up accurately along the full length of the line. With your forefinger and thumb spread apart as far as possible, press down firmly on the ruler. Figure 4-8 demonstrates how to prevent the ruler from moving as you score.

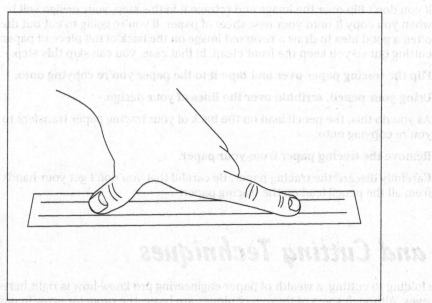

Figure 4-8:
Holding
down the
ruler.

2. **Run the point of an open pair of scissors firmly along the dotted/dashed line, holding the ruler in place.**

   You score dotted and dashed lines in exactly the same way. Hold the scissors as Figure 4-9 shows, lining them up with the edge of the ruler. As you draw the scissors across the paper, try to apply the right amount of pressure so the scoring crushes the card instead of cutting it. You may need to practice on some scrap card.

3. **After you complete the score line, create accurate folds.**

   For a valley fold, fold along the score line as a hill fold first; then fold the other way to make a valley fold. For extra crispness, fold the card over and run the back of a fingernail along the crease line.

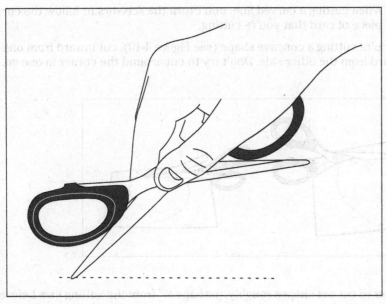

Figure 4-9:
Scoring with
a pair of
scissors.

Keen cutting

After you score the fold lines in your project (see the preceding section), you need to cut your paper. The key to successful cutting is accuracy. Take your time and try to cut right down the middle of the cut line. You need two different tools for cutting out the shapes in your templates (see Chapter 3 for more on tools):

✔ Scissors

✔ A sharp craft knife

Although these two tools are often interchangeable, each has its strengths. You get to know which tool to use in which situation with experience. This section explains how to cut using these two tools.

Cutting with scissors

Most of the time, you cut with scissors. They're fast, accurate, easy, and relatively safe. But the way you use your scissors depends on the material you're cutting and the type of shape you're cutting out. Remember the following tips to help make your cutting experience as easy as pie:

✔ **Thick card (over 300 microns or 12 thousandths of an inch):** For thick card, make only short cuts using the section of blade nearest the scissor's *rivet* (hinge). This gives you maximum leverage and makes the cutting easier.

✔ **Thin paper:** To cut straight lines on thin card or paper, make long cuts using the full length of the scissors' blades.

✔ **Curves:** When cutting a curved line, don't turn the scissors to follow the curve; instead, turn the piece of card that you're cutting.

When you're cutting a concave shape (see Figure 4-10), cut inward from one side; then cut inward from the other side. Don't try to cut around the corner in one go.

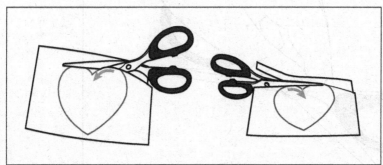

Figure 4-10: Cutting concave shapes.

It's often easier to cut out shapes roughly, perhaps ¼" from the cutting line, before completing the piece accurately.

Although you probably use scissors frequently in your daily activities, scissors are still a dangerous tool that can cause injury. Follow these safety tips:

✔ When they're not in use, leave your scissors with the blades closed away from the edges of your desk in a place where they can't easily fall. I keep all my tools on my desk in a plastic container, keeping them safe and easy to find.

✔ When carrying scissors, always hold them by the closed blades. That way, if you trip or someone bumps into you, they won't stick into anything they shouldn't. Don't run!

Cutting with a sharp craft knife

Some projects need a detailed cut. When you're cutting intricate or inaccessible shapes, such as the area in Figure 4-11, it's a good idea to cut along the tricky areas with a scalpel-style craft knife before you cut out the larger shape with your scissors. For example, you obviously need a knife to make cutouts in the middle of shapes.

To make a cut with a sharp craft knife, place the piece to be cut in the middle of a self-healing cutting mat and carefully cut out the shape. If you're super accurate, then the spare piece drops out as you pick up the card.

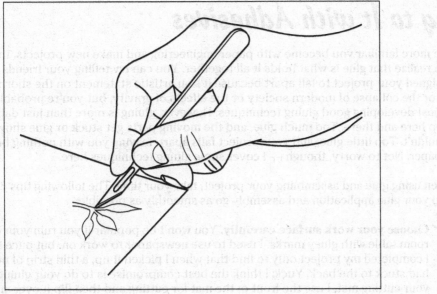

Figure 4-11:
Using a
knife to cut
paper.

Scalpel-style craft knives are sharper than you may think. They often use the same blades used in surgery, which means they're designed to cut through your skin easily. Trust me, and don't test it! To protect yourself, keep the following pointers in mind:

- ✔ **Keep the blade covered when the knife isn't in use.** Some knives come with plastic safety caps. When they don't, I make a quick sleeve to keep my sharp knives in. I take a strip of card (roughly 5" x 7"), wrap it around the knife a few times, fold the end over, and sticky tape it down.

- ✔ **Store the knife away from the edges of your desk so the knife can't fall and stick into your foot.** When I'm not using my knife, I keep the blade covered in the sleeve and place the knife in my plastic container on my desktop so that it's easily accessible.

- ✔ **Always cut away from yourself.** Make sure that your other hand is behind the blade. If the knife slips, it's much better to gouge the table than yourself. Turn the paper as needed.

- ✔ **Apply even pressure.** Using even pressure gives you more control. Don't press too hard — you're better off running over the paper with the knife a few times than trying to make a single deep cut.

- ✔ **Carefully replace and dispose of dull blades.** You have to apply more pressure to cut with a dull blade, so a dull knife is more likely to slip and create a jagged cut. Blades lose their edges quickly, so make sure you change them regularly. I usually change my blade every 30 to 60 minutes of work, depending on what I'm cutting.

  Blades can cut even after you put them in the trash, so dispose of your used blades carefully. I wrap my used blades in a sheet of paper and then tape it shut. That way, no one gets hurt, not even the garbage collector. Even better, you can place them in a screw-top jam jar (traditionally used in design studios).

Sticking to It with Adhesives

The more familiar you become with paper engineering and make new projects, the more you realize that glue is what holds it all together. You can try telling your friends that you designed your project to fall apart because it's an artistic statement on the shortness of life or the collapse of modern society or the effects of gravity, but you're probably better off just developing good gluing techniques. However, gluing is more than just dabbing a drop here and there. Too much glue, and the moving parts get stuck or glue shows where it shouldn't. Too little glue, and your project falls apart, leaving you with nothing but scraps of paper. Not to worry, though — I cover some gluing techniques here.

When using glue and assembling your project, take your time. The following tips can also help your glue application and assembly go as smoothly as possible:

✔ **Choose your work surface carefully.** You won't be popular if you ruin your dining room table with gluey marks. I used to use newspaper to work on, but once too often, I completed my project only to find that when I picked it up, a thin strip of newsprint had stuck to the back. Yuck! I think the best compromise is to do your gluing work on your cutting mat. I use the front of the mat for cutting and then flip it over and use the back of the mat for sticking. (Check out Chapter 3 for more on including a mat in your workspace.)

✔ **Choose the right glue for your materials.** Here's a quick guide:

   • Use white school glue on materials that absorb water, such as two pieces of paper or card.

   • Glue sticks aren't very strong, so they're not good for structural joints; use glue sticks for nonfunctional decorative adornments made of paper or card, not for complex models or pop-up mechanisms.

   • Solvent-based glue is for waterproof or shiny materials, so use it to apply googly eyes or similar items.

✔ **Keep your project free of stray glue.** Stray glue on the project immediately attracts dirt and spoils the clean look of your project.

✔ **Keep a chopstick handy when gluing.** It lets you get into places that are too small for your fingers.

✔ **When using white school glue, don't put too much glue on the joint.** Because the glue is water-based, if you use too much of it, the card gets water-logged and difficult to work with. Use a glue spreader such as a coffee stirrer to put a thin, see-through layer of glue on one surface.

✔ **Carefully join the pieces together with the glue in place.** While the glue is still wet, you can still make some small adjustments to the positioning. Make sure everything is lined up as accurately as possible. After you're happy with the positioning, pinch the parts together with your fingers or a pair of tweezers. Doing so fixes them in position.

✔ **Use solvent-based glue only in a well-ventilated area.** The fumes are toxic, so you need to use the glue in a large room with the windows and doors open. *Warning:* Be careful not to hunch over your work with your face too close to your project — you'll end up breathing in these toxic fumes before they even get a chance to ventilate. I found out the hard way. I used to do all my paper-engineering work in a box room at the back of our house until one occasion involving some spray-on glue that left me feeling decidedly woozy! Now I always make sure to have good ventilation for these gluing tasks.

✔ **Make sure you let the glue completely dry before carrying on.** The glue adheres fairly quickly, but it gets to full strength only after it has completely dried out. If you've used a thin layer of white school glue and pinched the paper together, the joint should be usable in only a few seconds and completely dry in a matter of minutes.

✔ **Store the glue in a safe place when you're not using it.** Small children and pets may be tempted to chew on white school glue and glue sticks. Kids can also find your solvent-based glues and end up gluing your fine china together in the blink of an eye, so keep your glues in a safe location. You can use a designated storage box or do as I do and store your glue with your other tools in a plastic desktop container.

Coloring Paper with Paints and Inks

Adding color to your paper-engineering projects can give them character and help them come to life. But waiting until your projects are complete before painting them usually isn't very practical. To prepare your paper before building the model or designing the project, you can make attractive patterned paper with the special techniques that follow. You can then use these papers to construct your own masterpiece. Just mark out the paper as you would with a plain sheet of paper. Experiment with your color schemes and see what you can create.

Not too much of a stretch: Helping wet paper dry flat

When you use water-based paint or ink on paper, you end up with wet paper. Normally, the surface of wet paper becomes uneven, but using the paper-stretching technique, you can keep your paper flat.

You need the following materials to stretch your paper:

✔ A newspaper to protect your work surface

✔ A shallow bowl of water (a large foil tray is ideal)

✔ A wooden board bigger than the paper you're stretching

✔ A piece of natural sponge

✔ Brown paper tape

✔ The paper you're stretching

✔ A ruler

✔ A sharp craft knife

Follow these steps to stretch your paper. You use the stretching process in combination with your coloring techniques. If you decide to use a watercolor wash (see the next section), you add the color after Step 4 of the paper-stretching process. If you prefer marbling inks (see the later "Marbling" section), you wet the paper during the marbling process, so you follow the stretching instructions starting with Step 4 here.

1. **Float the paper on the water in the bowl and let it soak for a minute.**

   Doing so lets the fiber in the paper expand slightly.

2. **Lift the paper out of the water and put it in the middle of the wooden board.**

   When you lift the paper up, let most of the water drip off before you put it on the board. Make sure that it's lying flat with no ripples or bubbles in the paper.

3. **Smooth the paper down with a clean sponge.**

   Start at the top of the paper and run the sponge across the width of the paper. Move down the paper and repeat the process; keep going to the bottom of the paper (see Figure 4-12). Doing so squeezes out any excess water and stretches the paper against the board.

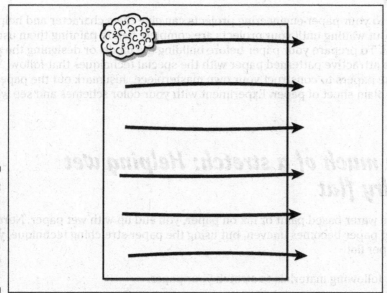

Figure 4-12:
Sponge across the paper to make sure there are no wrinkles.

4. **Wet some strips of brown paper tape and stick them down around the paper.**

   The strips need to be 4" to 6" longer than the width and height of the paper so that you have a good overlap (see Figure 4-13). The brown paper strips hold the paper in place as it dries. Without it, the paper dries bubbly.

   If you're adding a watercolor wash (see "Applying watercolor washes to your paper"), here's where you apply the paint.

5. **Leave the board lying flat while the paper dries out.**

   The paper takes a few hours to dry, but leaving it overnight is best. As the paper dries, the fibers shrink, making the paper tight. The end result is a nice, flat paper.

6. **Cut the paper from the board.**

   Use a sharp craft knife and ruler to cut the paper from the frame of the brown tape (see the earlier "Keen cutting" section). Put your newly stretched paper to one side. You need to soak the brown paper tape to get it off the board so you can use the board again.

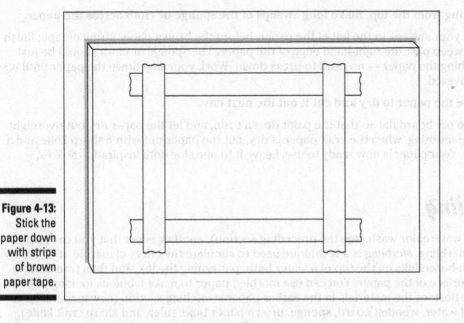

Figure 4-13:
Stick the
paper down
with strips
of brown
paper tape.

Applying watercolor washes to your paper

A *wash* is a simple but effective coloring technique that gives your paper an interesting colored finish. It's an even layer of watery paint that completely covers an area of paper, giving it a slightly textured color.

Besides the materials for paper stretching (see the preceding section), you also need the following:

- ✔ Watercolor paint
- ✔ A saucer
- ✔ A small piece of natural sponge or cotton cloth

To apply a wash to your paper, follow these steps:

1. **Follow the paper-stretching steps up to and including Step 4.**

   You should now have a board with a piece of damp paper stuck down to it.

2. **Mix your choice of watercolor paint in a saucer with water.**

   You can vary the amount of paint and water; experiment to find the effect you want.

3. **Dip the sponge or the cloth into the paint and allow the paint to soak in.**

   Use the sponge or the cloth to give you different effects — more time to experiment.

4. **Starting from the top, make long sweeps of the sponge or cloth across the paper.**

   Start your sweeps to the left of the paper, before the brown paper strips of tape; finish the sweep past the right-hand edge of the paper. The sponge or cloth should be just touching the paper — no need to press down. Work your way down the paper until it's all covered.

5. **Leave the paper to dry and cut it out the next day.**

   Leave the board flat so that the paint doesn't run, and let the paper dry out overnight. In the morning, when the craft paper is dry, cut the paper out with a sharp knife and a ruler. Your paper is now ready to use. Leave it to one side until inspiration strikes.

Marbling

Besides a watercolor wash (see the preceding section), another effect that you can apply to paper is marbling. *Marbling* is a technique used to simulate the effect of marble. It works by floating oil-based inks on the top of a water bath, patterning the ink, and then transferring it to the surface of the paper. You can use marbled paper to make fabulous looking paper creations. Besides the materials in the earlier paper-stretching section (newspapers, large foil tray of water, wooden board, sponge, brown paper tape, ruler, and sharp craft knife), you also need some marbling inks and a pencil. You can get these inks from your local craft store.

Follow these techniques to create some marbled paper:

1. **Soak your paper in your foil tray.**

   As soon as the paper has had time to soak through, set it to one side.

2. **Pick two or three colors from your marbling ink and put a few drops of each into the foil tray.**

   The inks are oil-based, so they float on the top of the water.

3. **Take a pencil and swirl it through the inks, mixing the colors.**

   Doing so makes a swirling marble effect on the top of the water.

4. **Lower the paper onto the water.**

   Start from one end of the tray. Lower the paper into the water. Try not to disturb the pattern as you do this.

5. **Lift the paper from the tray.**

   Lift the paper from the tray and place it face up in the middle of your wooden board.

6. **Complete the stretching process from Step 4 of the earlier paper-stretching section, finally leaving the paper to dry overnight.**

   With that, the marbling process is complete. After you cut out the paper, it's ready to use.

Part II

Going Flat Out: Commencing with Creative Paper Crafts

The 5th Wave — By Rich Tennant

HUNTER PUB
POP-UP BOOKS

"There's been an explosion in the pop-up factory!"

In this part . . .

In this part, I show you how to make some basic paper projects to whet your appetite for creating with paper. The crafts here take advantage of paper's flatness. You can hang them on your wall, tuck them into a bookshelf, or fold them flat, slip them into envelopes, and mail them to all your friends (and favorite writers of paper-engineering books).

This part starts with some layered cards that are easy to make. I then walk you through how to make pop-up pages and movable cards using a whole load of different paper mechanisms. I also show you how to combine your pop-ups to make more-complicated mechanisms and how to put pages together to make a pop-up book.

Chapter 5

Whipping Up Cards and Flyers, from Classy to Crafty

. . . .

In This Chapter

▶ Layering holes and cutouts

▶ Adding decorations

▶ Designing with decoupage and montage

. . . .

A greeting card is a fantastic way to send a message to someone you care about. No matter the occasion — thanks, congratulations, birthdays, and anniversaries — people enjoy receiving cards, and a handmade card with an added paper-engineering dimension is special because it lets the recipient know how much he or she means to you. Follow the simple techniques in this chapter to make a selection of classy and crafty greeting cards — as well as some posters or pictures for display. After you master these simple techniques, you can design your own inspirational projects. (For basic cutting, gluing, and scoring techniques, please see Chapter 4.)

Making Cute Cutouts

In paper engineering, making greeting cards is a matter of cutting, arranging, and mounting pieces of paper in a planned way. Making *cutout* greeting cards is the art of creating cards that use holes to make interesting and artistic spaces. Cutout cards have the following characteristics:

✔ They use holes and shadows to make interesting and attractive shapes.

✔ They can use a variety of different types and colors of card to make those shapes. (See Chapter 2 for more on paper and card.)

✔ You create them using sharp craft knives. Scissors are not good for cutting out holes.

After you have a design idea in mind, going from sketch to finished greeting card needn't be difficult. Just make sure that you know what you're aiming to produce. Cutout cards are easy and very rewarding. What better way to tell friends and family members how much you care than by giving them greeting cards that you spent time making with your own hands?

This section shows how you can use cutting techniques to make your own unique Valentine's Day card. Adding some embellishments, which I discuss in the next section, can give your card an even more original look.

Project 5-1: St. Valentine's Delight

A handmade card is the perfect message for your true love on Valentine's Day. This design is interesting because it uses several layers of card to make a 3D effect. Figure 5-1 shows an example of the finished product.

Tools and Materials

3 or 4 sheets of card (pink, dark pink, and red)	Sharp craft knife
Ruler	Cutting mat
Pencil and eraser	White school glue and glue spreader
Scissors	

1. **Copy the template in Figure 5-2 onto the pink card, score along the dotted line with a pair of scissors, and cut out the card.**

When you're drawing parts to cut out, draw them in reverse. After you cut them out, flip them over. That way, they'll be the right way around and won't have pencil marks all over them.

You need to use a sharp craft knife to cut out the hole, so be careful. Use the scissors to cut out the card.

Figure 5-1:
St. Valentine's Delight card.

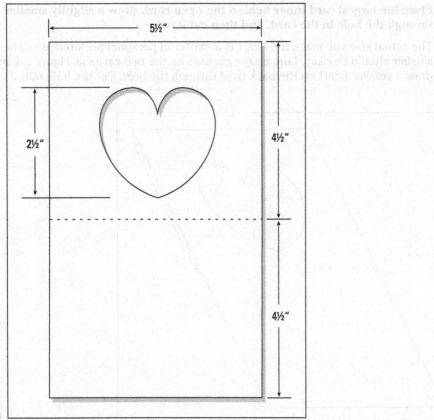

Figure 5-2:
Copy the template onto pink card.

2. **Copy the templates from Figure 5-3 onto red, dark pink, and pink card; score along the dotted lines so that the folds are crisp and accurate.**

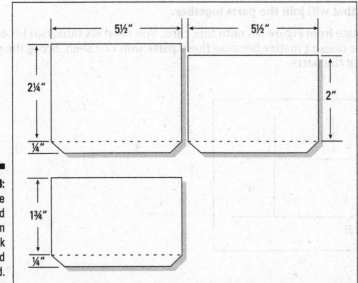

Figure 5-3:
Create these card inners from red, dark pink, and pink card.

3. **Place the largest card inner behind the open card, draw a slightly smaller heart through the hole in the card, and then cut it out.**

   The actual size you make the heart is a matter of personal preference — about $1/2$" smaller should be okay. Line up the creases on the two cards as Figure 5-4 shows and draw a smaller heart on the back card through the hole. Cut the hole out.

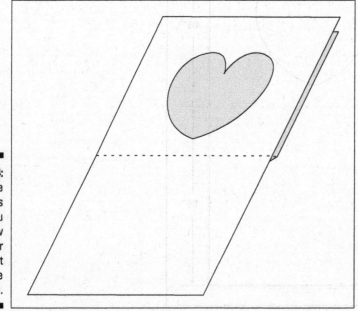

Figure 5-4:
Line up the two cards so you can draw a smaller heart through the hole.

4. **Repeat Step 3 with the middle-sized card inner**

   Line up the largest and medium-sized card inners. Draw a smaller heart on the medium card inner through the hole and cut the heart out. The smallest card inner has no hole..

5. **Make the tabs that will join the parts together.**

   Copy the template from Figure 5-5 onto thin card. You need six tabs, two for each card inner. The color doesn't matter because these parts won't be seen. Score the dotted lines and cut out the parts.

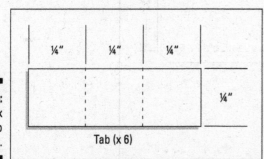

Figure 5-5:
Copy six tabs onto thin card.

¼"   ¼"   ¼"

¼"

Tab (x 6)

6. Glue the three card inners into place and let the glue dry.

Line the edge of the flap of the largest card inner with the crease in the center of the card and glue it into place. Glue the medium card inner behind the first, and glue the smallest card inner behind the medium one, as Figure 5-6 shows. Glue in the six tabs to complete the card.

Leave the card open to dry thoroughly. After it's dry, you can fold it flat. Write your message on the front and post it to your true love!

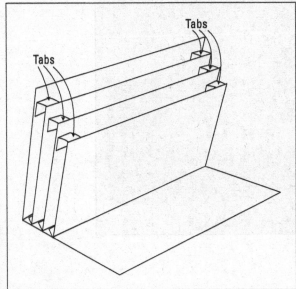

Figure 5-6:
Glue the card inners into place.

Embellishing with Attitude

Adding some embellishments to your greeting card can give it a unique look and feel. These decorative items, such as colored stickers or glitter, are the things that really finish off your design. You aren't limited in the types of embellishments you use, so look beyond the scrapbooking supplies and the paper aisles. Rely on your imagination; go with whatever fits your card's style.

A wide array of embellishments is available. Just visit your local craft store or scrapbooking store and search for different embellishments to accessorize your cards. Instead of just buying what you need for the project you're working on, see whether you can purchase lots of bits and pieces that you can keep in your toolbox. Look for ribbons, sequins, and so on, anything you can add to your creations.

When I visit my local craft store, I'm usually looking for bargains, but sometimes it's fun to splurge. Look at the more-expensive items, the specialty cards, and the handmade papers. Figure 5-7 shows the types of materials you may find. In addition to special types of card, you can often find little bits and pieces that add a touch of class (or a touch of bling!) to your cards. If you're lucky, you can find adhesive-backed ribbon, interesting shapes such as birds or flowers made from thin veneers of wood, stamps, and even sticky-back jewels.

By mixing these items, you can create your very own classy cards. Figure 5-8 shows the type of card you can easily create simply by sticking a few items together. You can also use these items to personalize a card. For example, if you're making a congratulations card for a couple who got married in Vegas, feel free to glitz it up with colored sequins and such.

Figure 5-7:
Check out
your local
craft shop
for some
of these
goodies.

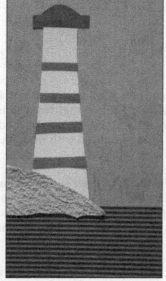

Figure 5-8:
Make your
own
embellished
card.

Cut and Mounted: Adding Layers with Decoupage and Montage

Montage and decoupage are both ways of sticking bits of colored paper onto a background. Prosaic as the process sounds, both of these techniques can produce fabulous effects. You can mix and match both techniques and create some wonderful paper creations. This section takes a look at them both and shows you what's possible.

With montage and decoupage, you cut out the individual parts of these pictures, so try to find pictures that are easy to cut. A bushy summer tree is easier to cut than a fiddly winter tree.

Bringing images together through montage

Montage, from the French word meaning "to mount," is a technique of sticking fragments of paper together to make a whole picture. The paper bits can be all sorts of things — bits of photographs, graph paper, musical scores, or just plain colored paper. Gluing these paper fragments onto a base sheet can make an interesting and unusual montage. Figure 5-9 shows an example of a finished montage.

Figure 5-9: Make montages by sticking all kinds of paper together to make a new picture.

Project 5-2: Montage Community Poster

A montage project is a fun and simple way to get your fingers wrapped around a paper-engineering project. Here I show you how you can quickly and easily make a poster for a community event using simple montage techniques. This poster is for a community coffee morning, but you can choose pictures and words that are suitable for whatever you're creating.

Tools and Materials

Magazine pictures and lettering for the poster

1 sheet of card

Glue stick or spray mount glue

Scissors

Sharp craft knife

Cutting mat

1 sheet of transfer lettering or text printed from your computer

1. **Choose pictures and text suitable for your poster.**

   You can find all sorts of pictures in magazines, and interesting fonts are often on the sides of packaging. Collect the parts that you need, including a picture you want to use for the background. Figure 5-10 shows the pictures that make up the coffee morning poster.

Figure 5-10: The parts for a montage poster.

2. **Cut out the background picture and glue it onto a sheet of card.**

   Doing so keeps the background rigid. Use a glue stick or, if you have it, some spray mount (aerosol) glue. Spray mount is expensive, but it's good for gluing large areas.

   Always use spray mount in a well-ventilated area.

3. **Carefully cut out the pieces from your magazines for the poster and arrange them into place on your poster without glue.**

   Experiment with the layout and positioning until you find one you're happy with.

4. **Glue the pieces into place to make up the poster you want.**

5. Add any final text to the poster.

You can either use transfer letters or print out some neat writing on your computer and glue it into place. Figure 5-11 shows the result.

After your poster is finished, you can take it to a copy shop to have multiple color copies made and then post them around the neighborhood or school.

You can create montage effects on your computer using programs such as GIMP or Photoshop (check out Chapter 14). Using the computer gives you more control of the finished montage and lets you use neat special effects, such as blurring or adding sparkle marks, which is difficult to do by hand.

Figure 5-11:
A poster
created
using
montage
techniques.

Adding depth: Decoupage that card!

Like montage, *decoupage* is another French word, this time meaning "to cut." 3D decoupage is a way of making pictures look three-dimensional by using multiple copies of the same picture. In the example decoupage picture in Figure 5-12, layers of the same picture are separated using double-sided sticky foam pads.

To make a 3D decoupage picture, you need a few simple supplies. Besides the usual paper-engineering tools such as scissors and a ruler, you also need multiple copies of the same picture. Decoupage uses these copies to make layers in the picture and give the impression of depth. You can buy actual decoupage kits from your local card shop, but making pictures from your own source materials is more fun. Look for inexpensive greeting cards, post-cards, or multiple copies of your own photographs.

Figure 5-12:
Decoupage pictures have a simple 3D effect.

Project 5-3: 3D Decoupage

You can make 3D decoupage with all sorts of subjects. For instance, you can make a decoupage project from a Christmas or holiday card bought from a card shop. This greeting card project, pictured in Figure 5-13, starts with a simple greeting card and makes it into a 3D picture that you'll be happy to display on your mantelpiece.

Figure 5-13:
A completed decoupage Christmas card.

This project uses sticky foam pads, which you can get from your stationery shop, usually near the sticky tape. They come in packs with a dozen sheets, each sheet with maybe 100 pads.

Tools and Materials

3 identical cards showing a scene you can easily cut out

Scissors

Sharp craft knife

Cutting mat

1 sheet of double-sided sticky foam pads

1. Plan your card's design.

Look for a card with a suitable subject. Find one that has three or four subjects on the card — for example, a couple of carolers and a Christmas tree.

Your card's design depends on what picture you're using. Look at Figure 5-14 to see the card I use this technique on. I've planned three layers for the picture and then sketched them so I know what I'm cutting out.

Figure 5-14: Planning your decoupage picture.

2. Cut out the parts for the different layers.

Use scissors where you can. For fiddly bits or holes, use your sharp craft knife. You end up with a collection of bits like those in Figure 5-15.

3. Stick the first layer of your picture into place.

Use the double-sided sticky pads to put the pictures into place. Stick the pads to the back of the new layer. Peel off the backing of the sticky pad and carefully stick the layer to the card, making sure that it's lined up accurately. Figure 5-16 shows what the result should look like.

Note: You can also separate the layers using blobs of thick silicone-based glue. Make sure you don't squash the glue when you build up the layers. You need to leave the glue to dry overnight.

4. Finish off the picture by adding the extra layer parts.

Use the sticky pads to fix the remaining parts into place. Make sure they're lined up accurately.

For smaller parts, you may need to cut the sticky pads into smaller pieces so that they don't stick out of the sides.

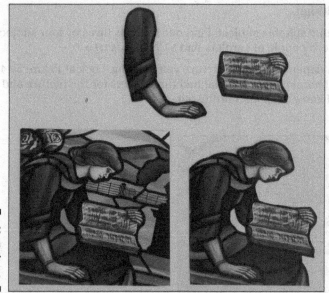

Figure 5-15:
Cut out the parts for your card.

Figure 5-16:
Stick the first layer into place.

Your decoupage card is now complete. You can use this technique to make all kinds of pictures on all sorts of scales. Try making decoupage from your own photographs or from prints of classical paintings. The layered effect and the shadows that the layers cast have a wonderful effect. Your pictures look really three-dimensional.

Chapter 6

Making a Pop with Your Pop-up

In This Chapter
▶ Adding depth to flat scenes
▶ Creating pop-ups that pop out toward you

Amazing but true, the very first pop-up books appeared more than 700 years ago. The first pop-ups were aimed at adults rather than children; they had moving wheels within wheels and were used to cast astrological charts. Instead of paper, they used *vellum*, which is a kind of leather that was specially treated to make a clean surface to write and draw on. Over the years, pop-up techniques have moved with the times.

Today's pop-up books are rather sophisticated, designed by artists to the delight of children as well as playful adults. Modern books often use paper or card, but you can use other materials to create unique effects. Pop-ups can pop up in a variety of ways. Some use a parallel pop-up mechanism, and some pop outward. Still others pop out with a single sheet of paper.

This chapter looks at the two main ways to pop your pop-up: parallel pop-ups and pop-out pop-ups. You need only a few basic tools and materials to make the simple pop-ups in this chapter: card, glue, scissors, a ruler, a cutting mat, and a sharp craft knife. You also need a little patience and bit of imagination. You can find details about the tools in Chapter 3 and about basic construction techniques in Chapter 4, but you have to look inside yourself for the imagination.

The Particulars of Parallel Pop-ups

The *parallel pop-up* is the classic pop-up: You open the page to reveal a scene with one or more layers in front of a background, giving the illusion of depth. Although simple, the parallel pop-up can be surprisingly effective, and the magic of seeing the apparently 3D scene appear from a flat greeting card is always a delight.

A parallel pop-up has the following characteristics:

✔ **Like all pop-ups, a parallel pop-up is able to fold down flat.** You accomplish this by placing two pieces of card parallel to each other. You can do this in one of two basic ways: the *cut* way or the *glue* way, which I discuss in the upcoming subsections.

✔ **The greeting card or book pages open to form a 90° angle.** To see the image pop up, you open the page only halfway.

✔ **It has two surfaces that are always lined up with each other.** Figure 6-1 shows an example. With a parallel pop-up, you essentially create a collapsible box, gluing the figure or character you want to pop up to the front face of that box. Here you can see that as the greeting card closes, the box collapses so that the back of the card and the character in front of the card area are always lined up, or parallel.

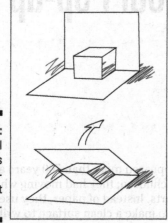

Figure 6-1: A parallel pop-up has two surfaces that line up.

This section walks you through a couple of projects to help you create your own parallel pop-ups.

Cut it out: A simple, sunny pop-up card

The *cut* type of parallel pop-up is perhaps the simplest type of pop-up you can make. With this type of greeting card, as the card is closed, an open-sided box folds down flat and is tucked away inside the card. When the greeting card is opened, the box unfolds as well, appearing to magically pop up before your eyes. Figure 6-2 shows three examples of the *cut* type of parallel pop-up.

Figure 6-2: Completed parallel pop-up greeting cards.

Birthday   New Baby   Happy Christmas

Project 6-1: Rising Sun Card

The Rising Sun greeting card is a great introduction to cut-style parallel pop-ups. In addition to using yellow and white card, you add some color with a picture from a magazine. Allergy medicine advertisements are a great source for sky and other outdoor vistas for this project.

Tools and Materials

1 sheet of thin white card	1 sheet of thin yellow card
Pencil and eraser	Drawing compass
Ruler	Scissors
Sharp craft knife	Magazine with a picture of the sky
Cutting mat	White school glue and glue spreader

1. **Using a pencil and ruler, mark the lines from the template in Figure 6-3 onto your card.**

   Be sure to mark fold lines as dotted or dashed and cut lines as solid.

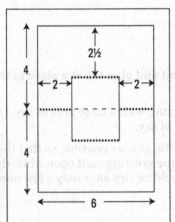

Figure 6-3:
The Rising
Sun card
template.

2. **Cut the two solid vertical lines with your sharp craft knife.**

   Place the card on your cutting mat, line up your ruler, and run your knife along the edge of the ruler. Don't cut toward yourself.

3. **Score the dotted and dashed lines with the point of an open pair of scissors.**

   Scoring, running the point of a pair of scissors along a crease line to dent it, gives your folds a crisp, professional look. Don't skip the scoring step. Refer to Chapter 4 for how to score your card.

4. **Carefully fold the card in half while also pushing the center piece so that it folds in the opposite direction from the main fold.**

   Pushing on the center piece changes the valley fold into a hill fold, creating a collapsible box.

   The pop-up should now fold flat. Check your greeting card by opening it. The center should pop up as in Figure 6-1. If it doesn't, make sure you push in the center piece in as you close the greeting card.

5. **Draw and cut out the sun from the yellow card.**

   Extend the points of the compass so they're 2" apart and draw a 4" circle. Draw some sun rays. Using your scissors, cut along the line you just traced to get your sun. You don't need the full circle, just the top $3/4$ as in Figure 6-4. Draw a line at about $1/4$ height and carefully cut along the line.

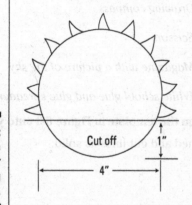

Figure 6-4:
Making the sun for your greeting card.

6. **Cut out a picture of the sky for the background and glue the sky piece to the top half of the open greeting card.**

Look through some old magazines to find a picture with a large area of sky. Using Figure 6-5 as a template, cut out a background of sky.

Spread the white school glue thinly, using as little glue as possible so that the sky doesn't wrinkle when you glue it down. Leave the greeting card open while the glue dries so that it doesn't all stick together. It should be dry after only a few minutes.

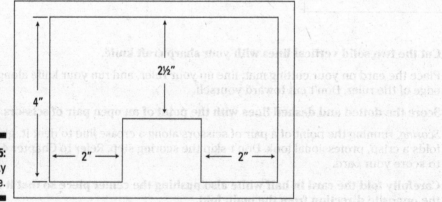

Figure 6-5:
The sky template.

7. **Glue your yellow sun into place on the front face of the collapsible box you created in Step 4.**

The sun should be centered on the greeting card and lined up with the crease at the bottom of the box (see Figure 6-6).

8. **Make sure the greeting card opens and closes freely.**

If bits are stuck down that shouldn't be, free them carefully with your sharp craft knife. You now have a pop-up sunrise. Simple to make but really rather effective, don't you think?

Figure 6-6: Completing your pop-up card.

The goodness of glue: A pop-up surprise

You can make parallel pop-ups without a knife, and I refer to them as *glue* type pop-ups. In this case, the picture you want to pop up and the back of your card sort of form the front and back of a collapsible box. A *picture tab* that goes along the bottom of your picture and a separate *top tab* that goes behind your picture form the bottom and top of that box. The sides of the box stay open.

The advantage of making your pop-up this way is that when the pop-up is closed, no signs give away that this is a pop-up; it just looks like a plain old folded greeting card. The disadvantage is that lining up your parts correctly is harder. Sometimes there's beauty in imperfection, but in this case, it can make it impossible to shut your pop-up, so measure carefully.

Project 6-2: Standing Castle Pop-Up

This design features a castle that stands up using a glue-style parallel pop-up. Keep your eyes open for other interesting subjects to make into pop-ups — maybe views around your district or simple shapes. Perhaps flowers or people you know. The possibilities are endless.

Tools and Materials

3 sheets of thin white card   Scissors

Ruler   White school glue and glue spreader

Pencil and eraser

1. **Mark out a sheet of white card with a castle and top tab (as Figure 6-7 shows).**

   The picture tab at the bottom of the castle and the center section of the top tab are both ¹/₄" wide.

2. **Score the crease lines on the top tab and the picture tab with the point of an open pair of scissors; then cut out the pieces.**

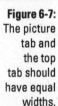
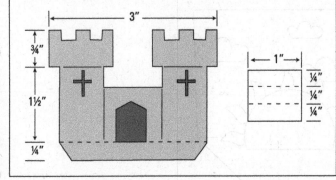

Figure 6-7:
The picture tab and the top tab should have equal widths.

3. **Fold a full sheet of white card in half, creating the main part of your greeting card.**

4. **Glue the picture tab down so that it touches the crease in the center of the open greeting card (see Figure 6-8).**

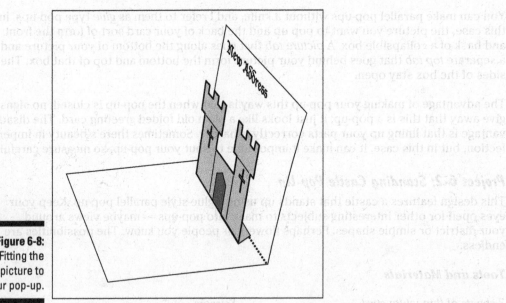

Figure 6-8:
Fitting the picture to your pop-up.

5. **Glue the top tab onto the back of the picture but not onto the greeting card.**

6. **Apply a little white school glue to the free end of the top tab and fold the greeting card so that it's closed with the tab stretched out toward the center of the pop-up.**
   Help make the glue stick by pressing down on the back of the pop-up where the glue on the tab is. Everything should now be nicely lined up. Figure 6-10 shows the proper placement of the top tab.

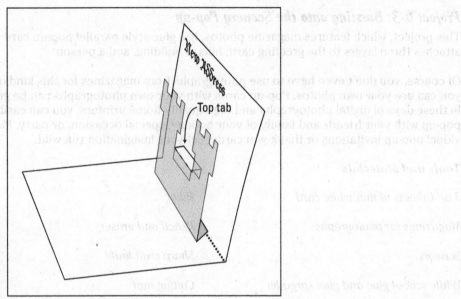

Figure 6-9:
Gluing down
the top tab.

7. Open and close the greeting card to check whether you've made it correctly.

Making your pop-up multilayered with photos

Your pop-up card doesn't need to have just a single layer. You can add lots of layers to give your greeting card a more complex look. Figure 6-10 shows a good example. This pop-up card has three layers, four if you count the greeting card itself. As the greeting card opens, it reveals the hills, a house, and a bear to complete the scene.

Figure 6-10:
A multilay-
ered pop-up
card.

Project 6-3: Bursting onto the Scenery Pop-up

This project, which features magazine photos, is a glue-style parallel pop-up card that attaches three layers to the greeting card: hills, a building, and a person.

Of course, you don't even have to use photographs from magazines for this kind of project; you can use your own photos. Pop-up cards with your own photographs can be great fun. In these days of digital photography and high-quality home printers, you can easily create a pop-up with your friends and family of your holiday, special occasion, or party. Make individual pop-up invitations or thank-you cards. Let your imagination run wild.

Tools and Materials

3 or 4 sheets of thin white card	*Ruler*
Magazines for photographs	*Pencil and eraser*
Scissors	*Sharp craft knife*
White school glue and glue spreader	*Cutting mat*
Glue stick	

1. **Fold a full sheet of card in half to make the main part of your greeting card.**

2. **Look through your magazines to find photos that can make a background for the greeting card, as well as the layers that pop up from it.**

   Find a hill that's as wide as the greeting card (approximately 8½") and about half as high. Find a building that's taller but not as wide as the hill. Find a person measuring between 4¾" and 5⅞" tall.

   Make the parts at the front shorter and/or narrower than those at the back so they don't block the view.

3. **Add a ¼"-wide picture tab to the bottom of the hill, building, and person; carefully cut out the shapes.**

   For complicated shapes, first cut close to the line you're aiming at — perhaps ⅜" away from it; then cut carefully on the correct line. Cutting out the picture is much easier if you're cutting near the edge.

   If your pictures are a little flimsy, try gluing them to a sheet of card with a glue stick before cutting them out along their edges.

4. **Create the top tabs.**

   1. On a piece of card, draw four 4"-long parallel lines ¼" apart.

   2. Score the middle two and cut the outer two lines.

   3. Cut pieces from this card to make your top tabs (see Figure 6-11). You need three or four of them for this project.

   The tabs are what hold everything in your pop-up card together. Don't make the tabs too long — ¾" should be fine. If they're too long, the parts of the pop-up will spill out of the closed greeting card.

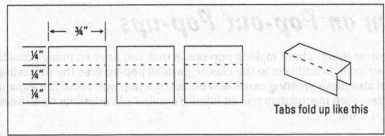

Figure 6-11:
Tabs for
the pop-up
card.

Tabs fold up like this

5. **Before gluing, place your hill, building, and person where you want them to be in the final project.**

6. **Using white school glue, glue down the picture tabs.**

   Line up each picture tab with the crease of the greeting card or with the layer before it. Be sure to space the magazine photos ¹⁄₄" apart to match with the ¹⁄₄" tabs. Glue the hill to the greeting card, then glue the building into place on the card, and lastly glue the person into place on the card.

7. **Glue in the top tabs and let your pop-up card dry.**

   Glue a tab behind each picture, connecting it to the layer behind it. Open and close the pop-up card to make sure it works. Keep your greeting card open when the glue is drying.

Now you're well equipped to do some experimenting on your own. You can have all sorts of fun with multilayered pop-up cards. Don't forget that you're not limited to one item per layer. One idea is to have a layer with two characters in front of a hill on each side of the pop-up card, as in Figure 6-12.

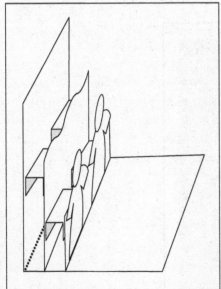

Figure 6-12:
A multilayer
pop-up
card.

The Lowdown on Pop-out Pop-ups

One of the greatest things about making pop-ups is that you have so many possible mechanisms to choose from. In addition to the classic parallel pop-up (see the preceding sections), you can also make greeting cards and books that pop out, twist, lift, expand, and swivel. Of course, each mechanism has an infinite number of variations on a theme, depending on what you want.

No matter whether you want bigger, smaller, wider, or taller; more movement or less movement; or subtle or garish, you can design a pop-up card for any occasion and for any theme (though I suppose that a sympathy card with pop-up daisies may be pushing at the boundaries of good taste!). This section shows you some of the different pop-up mechanisms that are available to you as a budding paper engineer, including info on how they work and how to modify them to suit your needs. Hang on to your tabletop — you're in for a pop-up ride!

Making a moving-mouth card

Using a few simple folds and moving parts, you can make a greeting card talk. Okay, perhaps actual speech is beyond the scope of paper engineering, but making moving mouths or opening and closing beaks is a breeze. All you need is a single slit and some well-placed score lines.

Project 6-4: Talking Frog Card

From fairy tales and jokes to singing puppets, talking frogs are a common theme. The following steps show you how to make your own version of a talking frog greeting card. Figure 6-13 shows what the completed moving-mouth card looks like. When you open and close the pop-up card, the mouth opens and closes in a delightful way. Ribbit, ribbit!

Figure 6-13
A completed moving-mouth card.

Tools and Materials

2 sheets of thin white card

Pencil and eraser

Ruler

Scissors

Sharp craft knife

Cutting mat

Glue stick

Colored felt-tipped pens

1. **Using a pencil and ruler, mark out the lines as Figure 6-14 shows.**

    Note that the solid lines are cut lines and the dotted and dashed lines are crease lines.

2. **Score along the dotted and dashed lines with the point of an open pair of scissors.**

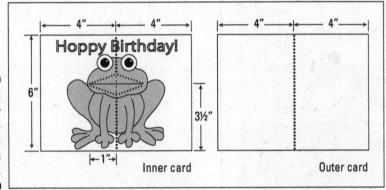

Figure 6-14:
Template for the moving-mouth greeting card.

3. **Carefully cut the solid lines.**

    Use your sharp craft knife to cut the slit in the middle of the card — this will be the opening of the mouth. Cut around the outline of the inner and outer cards; you end up with two identically sized greeting card pieces — one with a slit, one without.

4. **Draw your character onto the card, using the slit as a mouth.**

    The drawing is what transforms the simple slit into a mouth. Use colored pens or your choice of marking material (see Chapter 3) to draw your character onto your card. In the example, I've drawn a frog (Figure 6-14), but you may want to try a seasonal person — Santa for Christmas or Cupid for Valentine's Day. You may even want to try drawing one of your friends. If you're careful, you can even glue a photograph into place with the mouth appropriately cut.

5. **Fold the inner card in half while pushing the lips inward.**

   Doing so isn't as hard as it sounds. Look at Figure 6-15 for extra help. As you fold the card shut, push the lips inward from the back of the card. They fold neatly because you've scored the fold lines. Fold the inner card completely flat and run your fingernails over the crease lines to give a crisp, sharp crease. You can now open and shut the inner card a couple of times to try out the moving-mouth effect.

6. **Glue the inner card into the outer card.**

   Use a glue stick to put glue on the back of the inner card, avoiding the lips. With both card pieces open, glue the two parts together (see Figure 6-15). After the glue is dry, fold the pop-up card closed.

Figure 6-15
Finishing off the moving-mouth card.

 After you succeed making one moving-mouth card, you can easily adapt the simple design to suit other pop-ups. Try a really wide mouth (a wide-mouthed frog?) or a tiny mouth. Try varying the angle of the score lines at the top and bottom of the lips to give different effects. And the slit doesn't need to be a mouth. Why not make the opening part the lids of a winking eye? Or instead of using colored pens, you may like to try making the main character from colored paper. As always, let your imagination run riot.

Popping out with a single sheet

Using a single sheet of card and no glue at all, you can make simple but effective greeting cards. If you carefully choose the simple 3D shapes, the final projects can look attractive and quite complex. You do need to use a sharp craft knife, so make sure you check out the safety instructions in Chapter 4.

Project 6-5: O Christmas Tree! Single-Sheet Surprise

With only a series of curved cuts and some scored fold lines, this project creates a Christmas tree that pops out toward the viewer. Figure 6-16 shows the finished pop-up card. Experiment with cut angles and fold angles as you try designing your own pop-up card using this same technique. Start with something simple — perhaps a house — and see whether you can move on to a more-complicated model.

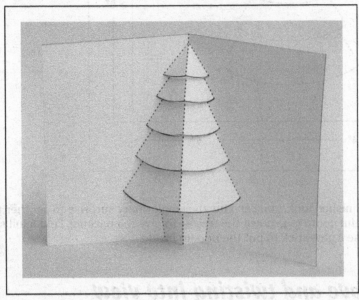

Figure 6-16: The single-sheet surprise.

Tools and Materials

1 sheet of thin white card	*Scissors*
Pencil and eraser	*Sharp craft knife*
Ruler	*Cutting mat*

1. **Using a pencil and ruler, mark out the card as in Figure 6-17.**

   Draw the curves freehand, trying to get them centered over the center crease.

2. **Score along the dotted and dashed lines with the point of a pair of scissors.**

3. **Cut all the internal cut lines with a sharp craft knife.**

4. **Fold the card in half and push the inner pieces toward the center as you do so (see Figure 6-18 to see the effect you're aiming for).**

   With the pop-up card folded closed, run a fingernail over the crease lines to make sure they're crisp and sharp.

TIP

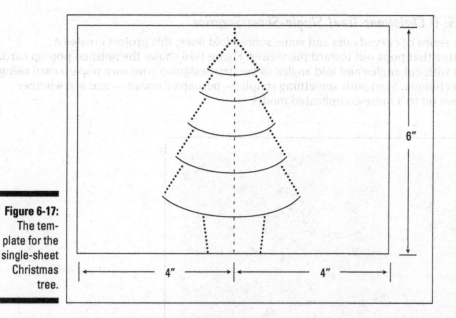

Figure 6-17:
The template for the single-sheet Christmas tree.

Note: For a more finished look, you can glue the single-sheet surprise to another piece of card — being careful not to glue down the tree — to give it a backing. Fold a full sheet of card in half and use a glue stick to put the pop-up inside.

Rising above and twisting into view

By careful use of angled creases, you can make scenes in which the subject of the pop-up twists into view. In this section, I show you how to make a simple pop-up that has this effect, using a kite as a subject. This technique features an outer card and an inner card with strategically placed score lines — you don't need any specially placed cuts.

Project 6-6: Soar-Away Kite Card

With this project, when the greeting card is closed, nothing is visible. Open it, and the kite, contained within, soars free of the boundary of the greeting card to hover over the top. You can use this simple mechanism for all sorts of fun pop-ups and pop-outs. Figure 6-18 shows what the completed card looks like.

This is a wonderfully flexible, simple, and effective mechanism. If you want to try a different variation, simply replace the kite with something else. Why not change the design by replacing the kite with a butterfly or a bird? Change the amount of movement by changing the angle of the crease lines, and change the position of the inner card to change the pop-out effect.

Figure 6-18:
The Soar-Away Kite greeting card.

Tools and Materials

1 sheet of thin white card

1 piece of thin colored card, 3¹/₂" x 3" or larger

Pencil and eraser

Scissors

Cutting mat

Ruler

Glue stick

White school glue and glue spreader

1. **Using a pencil and ruler, mark out the templates (see Figure 6-19).**

   Mark the inner and outer card pieces on the white card and draw the kite on the colored card.

2. **Score the dotted and dashed lines with the point of a pair of open scissors.**

3. **Carefully and accurately cut out the three pieces of card along the solid lines.**

   After cutting out the kite, save the scraps of colored card so you can later make the kite's tail.

4. **Fold the inner card in half while pushing the triangular section inward.**

   The triangular section at the top of the card is what does the work in this model. Figure 6-20 shows how to fold the inner card. After you fold the inner card flat, run your fingernails over the crease to make it nice and sharp.

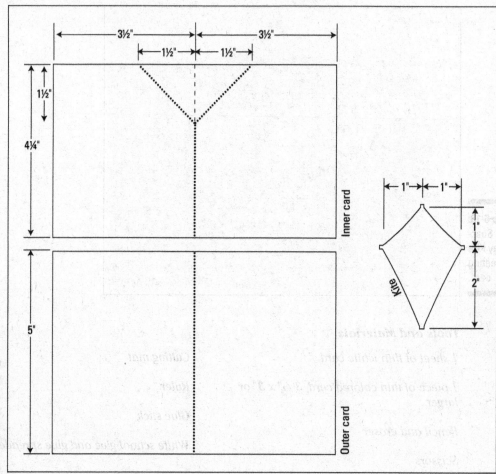

Figure 6-19:
The
templates
for the
Soar-Away
Kite card.

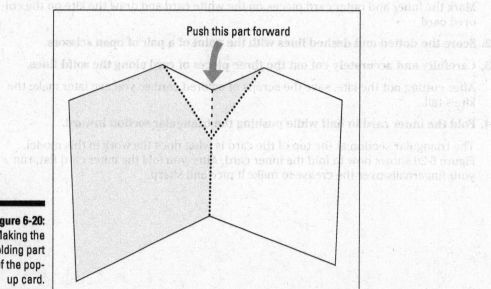

Figure 6-20:
Making the
folding part
of the pop-
up card.

5. **Use a glue stick to glue the inner card into the outer card, lining up the bottom edges (check out Figure 6-21).**

   Be careful not to glue down the triangular section at the top of the inner card.

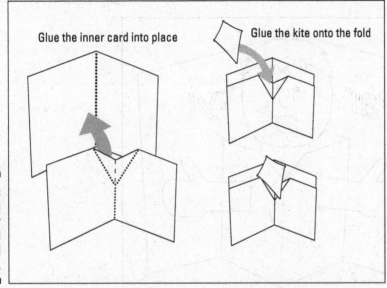

Figure 6-21:
Fitting the inner card and outer card together.

Glue the inner card into place

Glue the kite onto the fold

6. **Glue the kite into place with the glue stick (Figure 6-21).**

   You may need to reposition the kite so that it's hidden when the pop-up card is shut — do so before the glue dries.

7. **Cut three or four $^1/_{16}$"-x-3" strips of colored paper and glue them to the base of the kite using white school glue.**

   After attaching the kite's tail, leave your glue to dry with the pop-up card open. With the glue dry, your Soar-Away Kite Card is complete.

Mixing pop-up mechanisms

The fun thing about pop-ups is that you're not restricted to just one mechanism in each scene. For example, you can make one part of the greeting card pop in one direction and have another part pop in the opposite direction. Parts can move together or apart or even twist around each other as the pop-up card opens. In this section, I show you how to add a number of pop-up mechanisms to make a greeting card with character.

Project 6-7: A Card with Open Arms

Figure 6-22 shows the finished design of a greeting card with character. This pop-up card uses three separate mechanisms to make the body expand, the arms open, and the head lift up as the card opens.

Tools and Materials

2 sheets of thin white card   Sharp craft knife

Pencil and eraser   Cutting mat

Ruler   White school glue and glue spreader

Figure 6-22
A multi-mechanism card with character.

1. With a pencil and ruler, copy the templates from Figure 6-23 onto the white card.

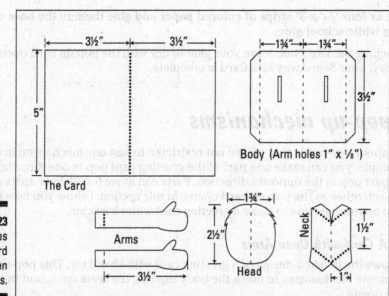

Figure 6-23
Templates for a Card with Open Arms.

The Card — 3½" + 3½", 5"

Body (Arm holes 1" x ⅛") — 1¾" + 1¾", 3½"

Arms — 3½"

Head — 1¾", 2½"

Neck — 1¾", 1½", 1"

2. Score along all the dotted and dashed lines on the card with the point of a pair of scissors.

3. **Cut out all the parts.**

   Carefully use the sharp craft knife to cut out the holes in the body. Use scissors for the rest.

4. **Glue the outstretched arms to the white card (see Figure 6-24).**

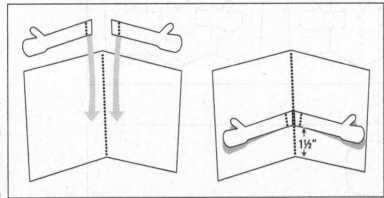

Figure 6-24:
Placing the
arms.

1½"

5. **Thread the arms through the holes in the body, and glue the body to the inside of the greeting card (check out Figure 6-25).**

   Fold the arms inward to fit them through the holes but flatten them out again after they're in place. Glue down the body. While the glue is still wet, close the greeting card completely and make sure that the body is lined up correctly. After it's lined up, open the greeting card and let it dry.

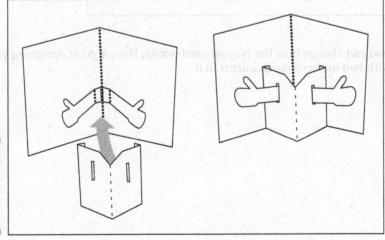

Figure 6-25:
Gluing the
body into
the greeting
card.

a

6. **Glue the neck piece at the top of the body as in Figure 6-26; then glue the head into place (Figure 6-27).**

   The neck piece attaches directly to the body piece. After your greeting card is complete, let the glue dry completely with the greeting card open.

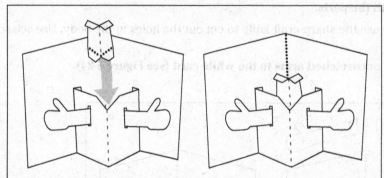

Figure 6-26:
Gluing on
the neck.

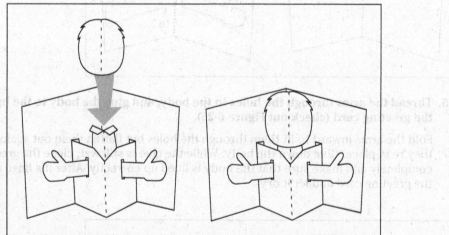

Figure 6-27:
Attaching
the head.

See whether you can change how the pop-up card works. Have a go at designing your own pop-up card with two or three mechanisms in it.

Chapter 7

On the Slide: Moving Along with Tabs and Wheels

You often find pull tabs in illustrated children's books, as well as in fun greetings cards. When my son was young, some of his favorite books were the books with action. Pull a tab here, and the hero's car drives across the page. Turn a wheel there, and a villain pops out from behind a tree. Turn the page to the next scene, and it's nighttime, dark silhouettes of skeletal trees hanging menacingly across the footpath; but pull the tab, and the scene changes. By clever use of interleaved slats, the dark footpath is gone, replaced by a dawn scene, and our hero safely completes his journey.

This chapter looks at the workings of flat mechanisms: pull tabs and wheels. I explain how to make simple pull-tab scenes so you can develop your own and amaze the children — young and old alike — in your life. I also go a step further, explaining how to make pages with two tabs and how to make simple animated stories.

Eyeing Practical Pull Tabs

Pull tabs are fun projects that come in many forms. Some tabs you pull so that a part of the picture on the page rotates; with others, you pull the tab and a paper door opens. Unlike a pop-up (see Chapter 6), a *pull-tab* picture doesn't move as you open the page. Only after you pull the tab does the fun start as the picture or card starts to move.

The more basic, practical pull-tab mechanisms have the following characteristics:

✔ **A tab to pull:** Usually at the edge of the page, you can easily find a small tab to pull.

✔ **Flat linkages:** In almost all cases, the pull tab needs a linkage. A *linkage* is a way to convert the straight-line motion of the pull into a circular motion or a motion in a different direction.

Within the limits of space, you can have as many tabs as you like on a single picture. Each tab moves or twists one or more parts of the page. Figure 7-1 shows a typical pull-tab project. Notice the tab at the bottom of the project and the heads, which are the moving parts of the picture.

Figure 7-1:
A typical
pull-tab
scene.

This section walks you through a couple of different types of basic pull-tab scenes to get you started on designing your own.

Making a linkage pull-tab project: Pull-tab pivot

A linkage is a really useful mechanism that you can adapt to a variety of uses. By carefully placing the parts, you can make your linkages turn one way or the other or even join linkages together to make complex movement. Through linkages, pull tabs can make parts of a picture move or turn, as I show you in the following project.

Project 7-1: Waving, Not Sinking

In this simple project, you create a linkage so that when you pull the tab, the character's arm moves back and forth as if he's waving (refer to Figure 7-2). Is the boatman waving at you or calling for help? Only you can decide.

Tools and Materials

2 sheets of thin white card	Drawing compass
Pencil and eraser	Scissors
Ruler	Cutting mat
Black felt-tipped pens	Sharp craft knife
Coloring pens	White school glue and glue spreader

Figure 7-2:
Pulling the tab lets the boatman's arm rotate, as though he's waving.

1. **Mark out the card as Figure 7-3 shows; draw the character in the boat with a black felt-tipped pen and color it in.**

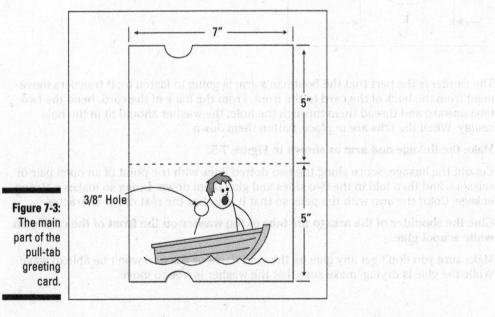

Figure 7-3:
The main part of the pull-tab greeting card.

Note that the hole needs to be circular. Use the compass to draw the circle approximately ³/₈" in diameter on the shoulder of the boatman.

2. **Using the point of a pair of scissors, score the dashed line.**

   Scoring means putting a dent in the paper where you want your crease to go. To score, simply drag the point of your open scissors along the crease line. See Chapter 4 for more info on scoring.

   The other half of the card will be folded over backward to hide the mechanism.

3. **Cut out the hole with the sharp craft knife.**

   Roughness in the cutting may make the mechanism catch and not work properly, so make sure that you cut the hole out neatly.

4. **Make a washer to fit in the hole (see Figure 7-4).**

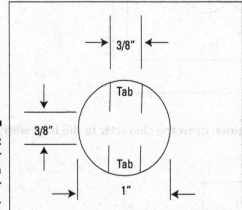

Figure 7-4:
The washer is a circle with four slits.

3/8"

Tab

3/8"

Tab

1"

The *washer* is the part that the boatman's arm is going to fasten to; it transfers movement from the back of the card to the front. From the back of the card, bend the two tabs upward and thread them through the hole; the washer should fit in the hole snugly. When the tabs are in place, flatten them down.

5. **Make the linkage and arm as shown in Figure 7-5.**

   Cut out the linkage, score along the two dotted lines with the point of an open pair of scissors, and then fold in the two sides and glue them down. Doing so makes a strong linkage. Color the arm with the pens so that it matches the rest of the character.

6. **Glue the shoulder of the arm to the tabs of the washer on the front of the card with white school glue.**

   Make sure you don't get any glue on the card itself, or the arm won't be able to wave. While the glue is drying, make sure that the washer is free to move.

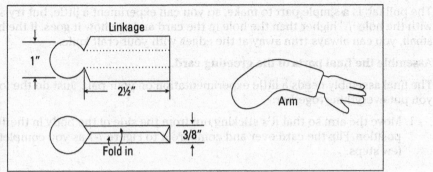

Figure 7-5:
The linkage
and the arm.

7. **Make the pull tab and sleeve, as shown in Figure 7-6.**

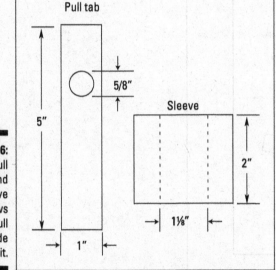

Figure 7-6:
The pull
tab and
the sleeve
that allows
the pull
tab to slide
through it.

The pull tab is the same length as the height of the card folded in half. This means that when the pull tab isn't being pulled, it sits flush with the bottom of the card. Although this is paper *engineering*, there's actually a lot of artistic interpretation involved. The hole in the pull tab needs to go slightly higher than the hole in the card.

The pull tab is a simple part to make, so you can experiment a little, but try starting with the hole $\frac{1}{4}$" higher than the hole in the card and see how it goes. If the hole is too small, you can always trim away at the edges with your craft knife.

8. **Assemble the final parts of the greeting card.**

The final assembly needs a little experimentation on your part. Just do the following as you put everything together:

1. Move the arm so that it's sticking out from the side of the body in the 10 o'clock position. Flip the card over and compare it to Figure 7-7 as you complete the next few steps.

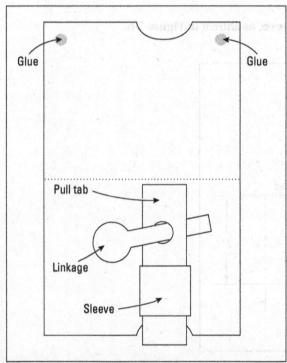

Figure 7-7:
A back view of the pull tab, sleeve, and linkage mechanism.

Glue

Glue

Pull tab

Linkage

Sleeve

2. Fold the sleeve over the pull tab so that the pull tab is free to move up and down. Glue the sleeve to the card, making sure that it's upright. The edge of the pull tab should be roughly $\frac{1}{2}$" from the edge of the paper washer.

3. Thread the linkage down through the hole in the pull tab and then glue the linkage to the washer. Make sure you don't glue the linkage or the washer to the card. While the glue is still wet, flip the card over and try gently pulling the tab to see whether you have the effect you're after.

9. **Fold down the back of the card and glue the two corners into place.**

Your pull-tab greeting card is now complete.

From this simple beginning, you can create a variety of designs. Try making a nodding dog design by gluing the head of your dog character to the washer mechanism. You can even make a more panicky looking sailor by having two arms waving in opposite directions: Make two washers and two linkages, one on each side of the pull tab, with both linkages going through the same hole.

Sliding-picture pull tabs

With pull tabs, the moving parts are endless. You can make a boy's arms and legs move, you can create a tree and have its limbs sway back and forth, or you can create a dog or cat with running legs. Just by carefully lining up holes and images, you can make a greeting card in which parts of the picture are animated. In this section, you discover how to use pull tabs and cutout viewing windows to move a picture.

Project 7-2: Paper Peepers Pull-Tab

The Paper Peepers project uses the sliding-picture technique to make a greeting card with shifty-looking eyes. Figure 7-8 shows what the finished project looks like.

Figure 7-8:
This pull-tab card lets the eyes slide side to side.

Tools and Materials

2 sheets of thin white card

Pencil and eraser

Black felt-tipped pen

Coloring pens

Sharp craft knife

Cutting mat

Scissors

White school glue and glue spreader

1. **Mark out one of your pieces of card.**

   Draw the character onto the card with black pen and color it in (see Figure 7-9). Use a pencil to draw in the score line.

2. **Use a sharp craft knife to carefully cut out the eye holes.**

   Make the eyes wide but not-too-high ovals so that they look sneaky!

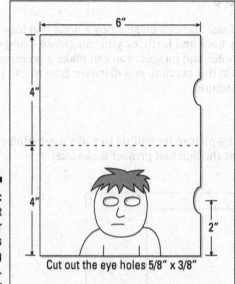

6"

4"

4"

4"

2"

Cut out the eye holes 5/8" x 3/8"

Figure 7-9: Marking out the Paper Peepers greeting card.

3. **Score the card and fold it in half.**

   Use the point of a pair of scissors to score along the dashed line before folding so that the crease is nice and sharp.

4. **Using your other piece of card, make the pull tab and sleeves (see Figure 7-10).**

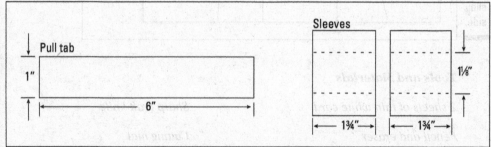

Pull tab

1"

6"

Sleeves

1⅛"

1¾"

1¾"

Figure 7-10: The pupils of the eyes will go on a pull tab bracketed by two sleeves.

The pull tab is the same length as the width of the card.

5. **Fold the sleeves around the pull tab and glue the sleeves to the back of the card.**

   The pull tab needs to go over the top of the eye holes. Glue the sleeves so that they're close to, but not over, the eye holes (see Figure 7-11).

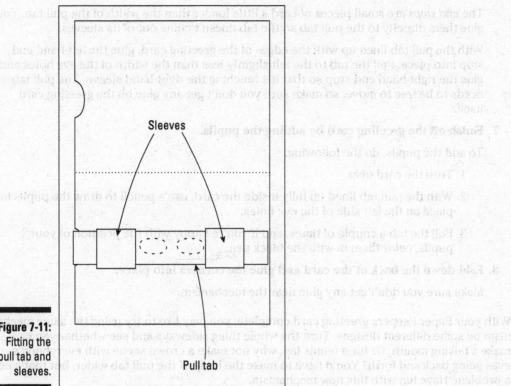

Figure 7-11:
Fitting the pull tab and sleeves.

6. Glue two end stops onto the pull tab (Figure 7-12).

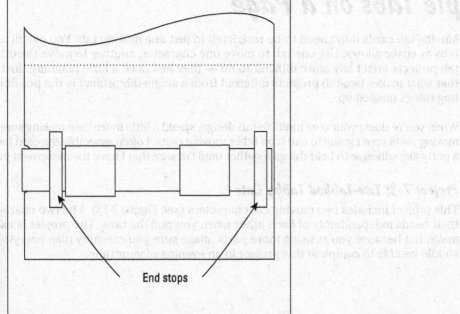

Figure 7-12:
The end stops keep the pull tab from moving too far.

The *end stops* are small pieces of card a little longer than the width of the pull tab. You glue them directly to the pull tab so the tab doesn't come out of its sleeves.

With the pull tab lined up with the edges of the greeting card, glue the left-hand end stop into place. Pull the tab to the left slightly less than the width of the eye holes and glue the right-hand end stop so that it's touching the right-hand sleeve. The pull tab needs to be free to move, so make sure you don't get any glue on the greeting card itself.

7. **Finish off the greeting card by adding the pupils.**

    To add the pupils, do the following:

    1. Turn the card over.

    2. With the pull tab lined up fully inside the card, use a pencil to draw the pupils in place on the left side of the eye holes.

    3. Pull the tab a couple of times, and if you're happy with the position of your pupils, color them in with the black pen.

8. **Fold down the back of the card and glue the corners into place.**

    Make sure you don't get any glue near the mechanism.

With your Paper Peepers greeting card complete, you may like to try using the same mechanism on some different designs. Turn the whole thing sideways and see whether you can make a talking mouth. Or for a tennis fan, why not make a crowd scene with everybody's eyes going back and forth? You'd have to make the body of the pull tab wider, but that's not a problem. Have fun with this new mechanism.

Two Tabs Are Better Than One: Putting Multiple Tabs on a Page

Moving-tab cards don't need to be restricted to just one moving tab. You can fit as many tabs as space allows. Use one tab to move one character, another to move the other. Two-tab projects aren't any more difficult to do — they just need a little planning. Just remember that what makes two-tab projects different from a single-tab project is the possibility of getting things tangled up.

When you're doing your own multiple-tab design, spend a little more time making sure that any moving parts aren't going to catch on other moving parts. I often assemble the card loosely using a putty-like adhesive to hold things together until I'm sure that I have the movement just right.

Project 7-3: Two-Tabbed Tabby Cats

This project includes two moving cat characters (see Figure 7-13). The two characters move their heads independently of each other when you pull the tabs. The project is easy to make, but because you're using more parts, make sure you carefully plan everything. You should be able to complete this project in an evening of your time.

Tools and Materials

2 sheets of thin white card

Pencil and eraser

Black felt-tipped pen

Coloring pens

Sharp craft knife

Cutting mat

Scissors

White school glue and glue spreader

Figure 7-13: Using two tabs to move two different kitty cats.

1. Take a full sheet of card and mark it up as shown in Figure 7-14.

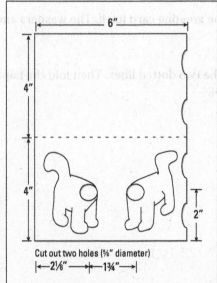

Figure 7-14: The template for the Tabby Cats card.

6"

4"

4"

2"

Cut out two holes (⅝" diameter)

|← 2⅛" →|← 1¾" →|

Note that the dashed line is a score line at half the height of the card; it lets you easily fold the card in half.

2. **Draw the two cat bodies on the card with a pencil and color them in with pen when you're happy with them.**

   If you really want to make tabby cats, don't forget that tabby cats are stripy.

3. **Cut out the two holes with a sharp craft knife.**

   Take care to cut the holes out neatly; jagged edges stop the mechanism from working properly.

4. **Make two heads and two washers (see Figure 7-15).**

   Use a sharp craft knife to cut the inner tabs of the washers. You can cut the rest out with your scissors.

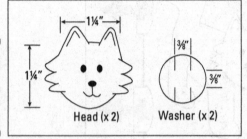

Figure 7-15: The kitties' heads and the washers.

Head (x 2)   Washer (x 2)

Color the heads in the same way as the bodies so they match.

5. **Fit the washers into the card.**

   Fold up the two tabs on each washer. From the back of the card, thread the tabs through the holes then fold them flat.

6. **Glue the kitties' heads to the tabs of the washers.**

   Make sure you don't get any glue on the greeting card itself. The washers and heads must be able to turn freely.

7. **Make the linkages (see Figure 7-16).**

   Cut out each linkage and score along the two dotted lines. Then fold the flaps over and glue them down to make a strong linkage.

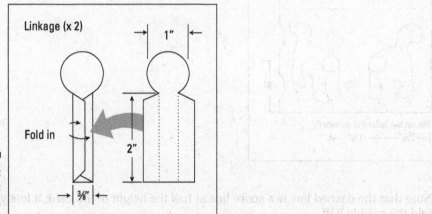

Linkage (x 2)

1"

Fold in

2"

⅜"

Figure 7-16: The linkages.

The next part of the instructions are basically the same for both cats. After you complete the mechanism for one cat, repeat the process for the second one.

8. Make a pull tab and sleeve (see Figure 7-17).

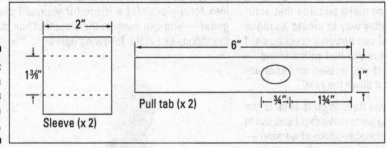

Figure 7-17: Making the pull tabs and the sleeves.

Sleeve (x 2)

Pull tab (x 2)

Each pull tab is the same length as the width of the card. The hole in the pull tab should be slightly wider than the width of the shaft on the linkage. With the pull tab lined up with the sides of the card, the hole in the pull tab should be aligned with the hole where the cat's head sits.

9. Fit the pull tab to the card and glue down the sleeve (see Figure 7-18).

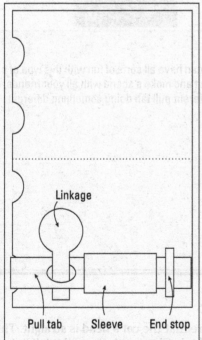

Figure 7-18: Gluing the tab sleeve into place.

Linkage

Pull tab   Sleeve   End stop

Wrap the sleeve around the pull tab. Glue the sleeve to the back of the card about ¹/₂" below and to the right of the hole where the head goes. Glue an end stop, a piece of card a little longer than the width of the pull tab, directly to the tab, to the right of the sleeve. Make sure you leave some space between the sleeve and the end stop so the tab can move.

A photographic memory: Moving photo projects

Having photographs of your friends is great, but what's even better is bringing those photos to life. By using pull-tab techniques, you can make pictures that actually move. In fact, what better way to create a unique birthday or holiday gift? You can design a greeting card showing a shared experience you had with a friend — perhaps the time the two of you missed an important bus, with you both chasing it down the road.

To do a photo project, all you have to do is stick to the basic techniques for making parts move that I discuss in this chapter. Simply find a suitable photo of a friend — you need two copies. Carefully cut out the head from one of the photographs. On the other copy of the photograph, make a washer, pull tab, and linkage so you can make your friend shake his or her head as if dancing. The following figure shows you an example.

Feel free to experiment and make your own photograph pull-tab project. If you want to be even more creative, look for a picture of a friend (or yourself) playing the guitar — you can animate the picture of him strumming the strings like in the following figure.

You can have all sorts of fun with this type of project. Go all out and make a scene with all your friends, each with a different pull tab doing something different.

DANCING DUMMY

10. **Fit the linkage and glue it to the washer.**

 Looking at the front of the card, make sure that the cat's head is straight. Thread the linkage down through the hole in the pull tab. Then, with the pull tab lined up with the edge of the greeting card, glue the linkage to the back of the washer.

11. **Repeat Steps 7 through 9 with the other pull tab on the other cat head (see Figure 7-19).**

 This time the pull tab goes above the hole in the card and the sleeve is to the left of the linkage. You also don't need an end stop because the linkage prevents the pull tab from pulling out of the card.

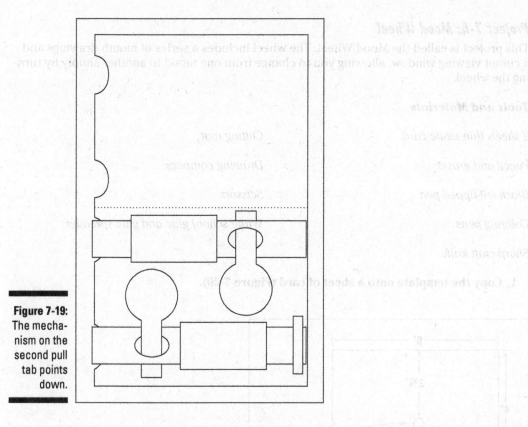

Figure 7-19:
The mechanism on the second pull tab points down.

12. **Use a couple of small dots of glue on the back of the card to hide the mechanism.**

Rolling Out the Wonder of Wheels

A paper washer lets parts of your card rotate freely. With a single or double pull-tab project, you create the washer to hold other parts — such as a nodding head or waving arm — to the card (see the earlier section titled "Making a linkage pull-tab project: Pull-tab pivot"). But you can take your projects in another direction by changing the washer.

With a wheel project, you change a washer into a larger wheel. Basically, to do so, you just increase the size of the washer but leave the tabs just a little larger. A full-size wheel can have all kinds of uses in your moving card — everything from a swirling pattern to dazzle your eyes to a secret code-cracking wheel.

The main characteristics of a wheel project are as follows:

✔ **A wheel almost as large as the page:** Tabs hold a large wheel in place so it's free to turn.

✔ **One or more cutout viewing holes in the main card:** You use holes so that most of the wheel stays covered. As you turn the wheel, parts of it are revealed.

Project 7-4: Mood Wheel

This project is called the Mood Wheel. The wheel includes a series of mouth drawings and a cutout viewing window, allowing you to change from one mood to another simply by turning the wheel.

Tools and Materials

2 sheets thin white card

Pencil and eraser

Black felt-tipped pen

Coloring pens

Sharp craft knife

Cutting mat

Drawing compass

Scissors

White school glue and glue spreader

1. **Copy the template onto a sheet of card (Figure 7-20).**

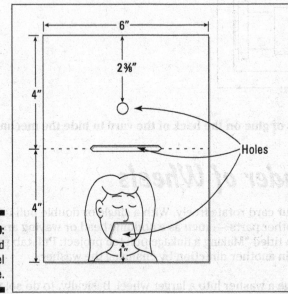

Figure 7-20:
The Mood
Wheel
template.

Use a pencil to draw a character based on the picture in the template onto the card. When you're happy with the drawing, color the picture with the coloring pens and draw around it in black pen.

2. **Cut out the three holes with the sharp knife.**

3. **Create the wheel.**

Using the compass, draw the wheel onto the second piece of card (see Figure 7-21). Mark out the two tabs in the circle's center, cut around the tabs, and cut out the wheel.

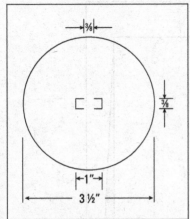

Figure 7-21:
Making the
wheel.

4. **Using the two tabs, fit the wheel into place in the hole on the back of the card.**

   When you close the card, the edge of the wheel should stick slightly out of the long hole at the fold of the card. You may need to make the long hole bigger to make sure that it fits properly.

5. **Draw different mood faces on the mood wheel.**

   Draw the different sets of mouths onto the wheel through the hole in the front of the card. Draw one mouth, turn the wheel until it's fully hidden, and then draw another mouth. Repeat this process until there's no more room on the wheel. Check out some ideas for different expressions in Figure 7-22.

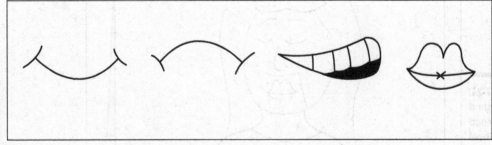

Figure 7-22:
Make as
many moods
as you want.

6. **Use a couple of small dots of glue to seal the card shut.**

7. **Cut a small circle of card and glue it to the tabs sticking out of the back of the card (see Figure 7-23).**

   Make sure you don't get any glue onto the card itself so the wheel is always free to turn.

Your Mood Wheel is now complete (see Figure 7-24). You can use the wheel mechanism to create your own designs. Try making a message card to hang on your bedroom door. In the window, you can show different messages: *Sleeping, Do not disturb, Out partying!* and so on.

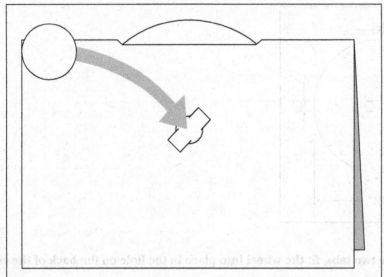

Figure 7-23:
Securing
the wheel.

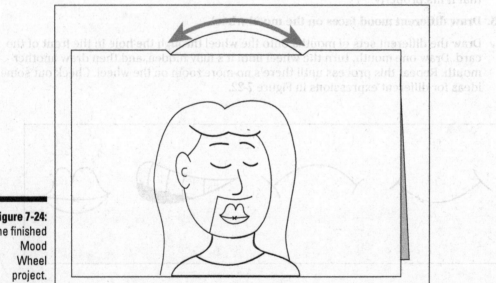

Figure 7-24:
The finished
Mood
Wheel
project.

Chapter 8

Mixing It Up! Pop-ups, Pull Tabs, and Cross-Fades, All in One

. . . .

In This Chapter

▶ Transitioning from one picture to another

▶ Putting together a series of pages

. . . .

As for pop-ups and other flat mechanisms, you have loads of options you can use in your paper creations. You can use tabs that make things move (as in Chapter 7), mechanisms that make shapes appear when you open the card (as in Chapter 6), and even pull tabs that cause one picture to fade into another. But your creations aren't limited to one mechanism; you can add two or more of these mechanisms to make a really interesting moving picture.

If you want to experiment and mix it up, you've come to the right place. This chapter shows how to combine pictures using a single mechanism and how to use different types of mechanisms in a pop-up book.

Before you try designing your own cards and books, spend a little time making up some of the projects here so you get a good understanding of how these models work.

Putting Two Pictures in One with a Cross-Fade

Why give people just one picture when you can give them two? The *cross-fade* mechanism allows you to present two entirely separate pictures, using a set of interlocking leaves to let viewers transition from one picture to another. For example, in the center of the page, maybe you see an evening street scene: The sun is setting over the horizon, and the houses are bathed in an orange glow. Pull the tab at the side of the card, and darkness falls: The sky is black, with only the moon and a few stars lighting it up. In the houses, the windows are lit from within. Night has fallen.

Project 8-1: Cross-Fade Picture

When creating a cross-fade mechanism, the pictures can be of anything. Go from a stormy sea to a calm sea, day to night, anything you like. Pull the tab, and one picture fades into the other; push the tab back to return to the original picture. Here are some basic instructions on creating your own cross-fade.

Tools and Materials

2 sheets of thin white card

Ruler   *Cutting mat*

Pencil and eraser   *Scissors*

Black and colored pens to complete your *White school glue and glue spreader*
illustration

Sharp craft knife

1. **Copy the two templates from Figure 8-1 onto thin card.**

   Accuracy is essential for cross-fade mechanisms, so be as accurate as you can when drawing the parts onto your card to ensure the model works as well as possible.

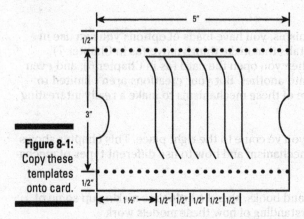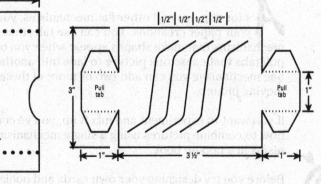

Figure 8-1:
Copy these
templates
onto card.

2. **Score the parts, draw your scenes on the back of each piece, and cut along the solid lines.**

   Before you make the parallel cuts in the card, draw your two scenes on the backs of the pieces (on the sides without the cut lines) and color them in as you like. Make sure your drawing is on the back. After you complete the coloring, flip the card over and cut along the slat lines with the sharp craft knife. Cut out the pieces with a pair of scissors.

3. **Glue down the flaps of the piece with the slits in it to make strong pull tabs.**

4. **Thread the slats from one piece up through the slits in the other piece.**

   This job can be quite fiddly because you need to have a hold of several separate pieces of paper as you fit everything together. If you can't grow an extra arm (which is tough if you aren't a starfish), try enlisting some willing help. Figure 8-2 shows you what to do.

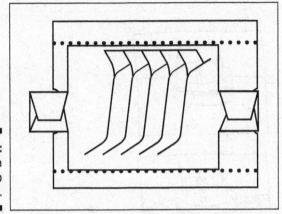

Figure 8-2:
Thread the slats into place.

5. **Fold the top and bottom flaps over and glue them to the piece with the slats.**

   If glue gets in the wrong place, the cross-fade won't work. Don't get any glue on the piece of card with the slits in it. Use as little glue as possible and make sure none of it gets into the mechanism.

   Figure 8-3 shows how to glue the flaps to the piece with the slats. With the flaps glued down, all the parts should hold together.

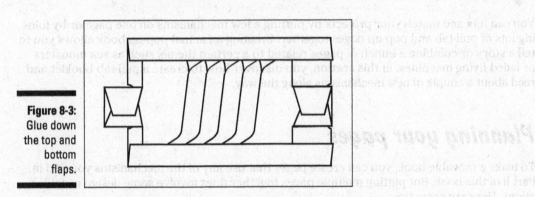

Figure 8-3:
Glue down the top and bottom flaps.

6. **Flip the card over and test the completed creation.**

   The pictures are on the other side of the card, so turn the card over and have a look. Pull and push the tabs on the sides of the card to fade from one scene to the other.

   After you master this mechanism, you can used it for all sorts of projects, like the ones in Figure 8-4. Perhaps create a birthday card: Pull the tab to reveal a happy birthday message. Or use the cross-fade to show different channels on a TV: You can create a mask to go over the top of the picture in the shape of a TV.

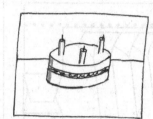

Figure 8-4:
Try these ideas with your cross-fade mechanism.

Making Movable Books

You can mix and match your projects by putting a few mechanisms on one page or by joining lots of pull-tab and pop-up pages together. Creating an actual pop-up book allows you to tell a story or combine a bunch of pages related to a certain theme, such as sea monsters or failed flying machines. In this section, you discover how to create a pull-tab booklet and read about a couple of new mechanisms along the way.

Planning your pages

To make a movable book, you can create pages that use any of the mechanisms you find in Part II of this book. But putting multiple pages together does involve some design considerations. Here are some tips:

- Choose the right mechanisms for the movements you want. Ask yourself how you want the pop-up or pull-tab mechanism to move. Spend a little time brainstorming about what kind of movement makes sense for your subject or story.

- Remember that each page needs to be the same size so the pages fit together to make a book.

- Think about where you'll connect the pages. If all the pages attach at the left, you can't put any pull tabs or wheels on the left-hand side of a page.

- Consider how you'll put the book together. I assemble my booklets by adding a flap to each page and using those flaps to glue the pages together. You may want to include a cover to give your project a real book feel.

Project 8-2: A Slightly Cheesy Mouse Story

The project in this section shows you how you can join one or more pages to make a small pop-up book. First you need some pages. Figure 8-5 shows the short story that the sample book contains. On the first page, our hero pokes his nose out of his mouse hole. He smells something tasty! In the second frame, he sniffs at the cheese, twitching his nose. And in the final frame, he jumps for joy.

Figure 8-5: The three pages of the mouse story.

The first and last pages use completely new mechanisms, but the middle page uses a modified version of one from Chapter 7.

For each of the three pages, you need the following tools and materials. The upcoming sections break down how to create these three pages and assemble them into the final project.

Tools and Materials

2 or 3 sheets of thin white card	*Scissors*
Ruler	*White school glue and glue spreader*
Pencil and eraser	*Black and colored pens to complete your illustration*
Sharp craft knife	
Cutting mat	

Slider mechanism: Page one, the mouse comes out of the hole

The *slider mechanism* pulls a character either across the page or up and down the page. The card has two parallel slits in it, and you thread another piece of card through the slits. The longer the slits, the farther the character moves. You can use the slider mechanism for a wide variety of designs: a car driving across the page, a rocket launching, or as in this project, a mouse peeping out of his hole.

Follow these instructions to make the sliding mechanism for the first page of the booklet:

1. **Copy the template from Figure 8-6 onto a sheet of thin card.**

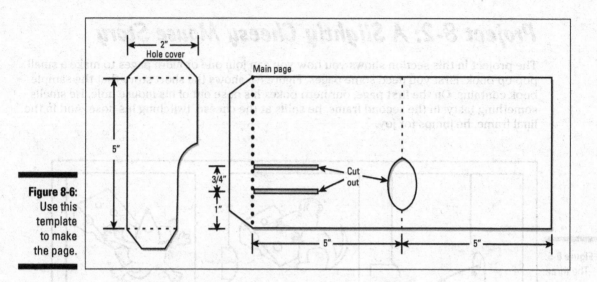

Figure 8-6:
Use this template to make the page.

2. **Score along the dotted and dashed lines and cut out the hole and slits with a sharp knife; then use scissors to cut out the pieces.**

3. **Copy the pull tab and mouse head from Figure 8-7 onto a second piece of card.**

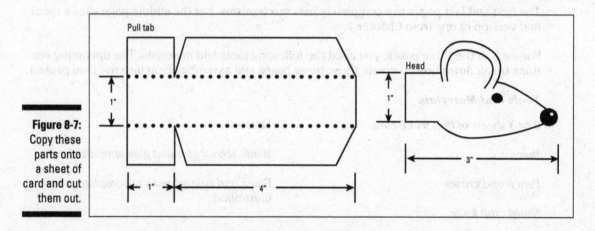

Figure 8-7:
Copy these parts onto a sheet of card and cut them out.

4. **Score any dotted lines and cut out the parts.**

5. **Fold the long flaps of the pull tab around and glue them down.**

    Don't glue down the short tabs; leave them pointed upward, as Figure 8-8 shows.

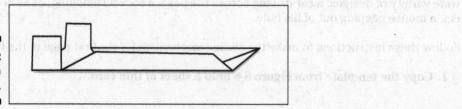

Figure 8-8:
Assemble the pull tab.

6. Thread the two tabs from the pull tab up through the two slits in the page.

Figure 8-9 shows what to do. Fold the two tabs over and glue them together so they make a flat surface to glue the mouse's head onto. Make sure you don't get any glue on the page — the parts have to be free to move.

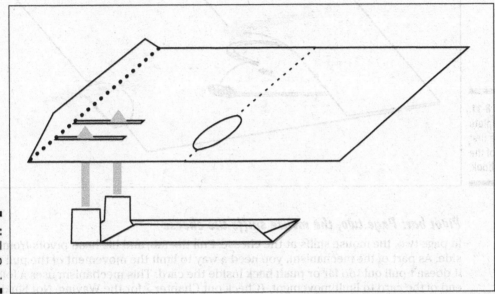

Figure 8-9:
Fit the pull tab into place.

7. Glue the head and the hole cover into place (see Figure 8-10).

The mouse head glues onto the pull tab. When you pull the tab, the mouse head moves. Glue the hole cover into place over the top of the page. The tabs at the top and bottom glue onto the back of the page.

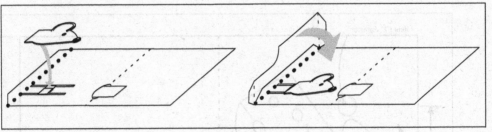

Figure 8-10:
Glue the head and the cover into place.

8. Fold the right-hand side of the card around and glue it into place.

You need only a couple of dots of glue to hold the back of the card down. Figure 8-11 shows the completed page. Set the page to one side while the glue dries.

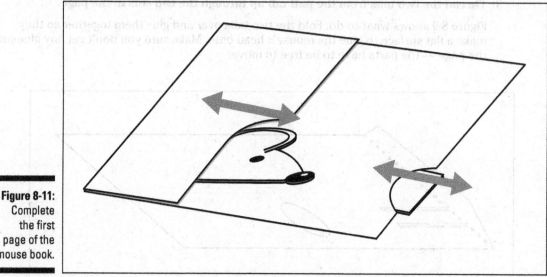

Figure 8-11:
Complete
the first
page of the
mouse book.

Pivot bar: Page two, the mouse sniffs the cheese

In page two, the mouse sniffs at the cheese. Pull the tab, and his head pivots from side to side. As part of the mechanism, you need a way to limit the movement of the pull tab so that it doesn't pull out too far or push back inside the card. This mechanism uses a fold at the end of the card to limit movement. (Check out Chapter 7 for the Waving, Not Sinking project, which shows a similar mechanism that uses slider sleeves and end stops to limit movement. *Slider sleeves* are the pieces that the pull tab fits into; they keep the pull tab correctly aligned while allowing it to move. *End stops* prevent the pull tab from moving too far.)

Here's how to make page two of the mouse's story:

1. **Copy the template from Figure 8-12 onto a sheet of thin card.**

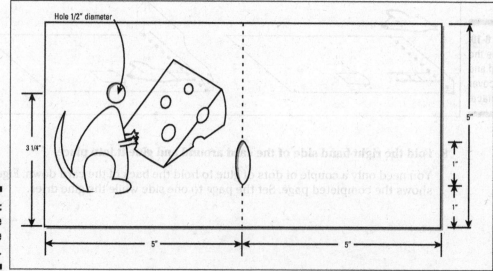

Figure 8-12:
Copy the
template
onto card.

2. **Score along the dotted lines and cut out the holes with a sharp craft knife.**

3. **Copy the remaining parts from Figure 8-13 onto thin card and color the pieces as you like.**

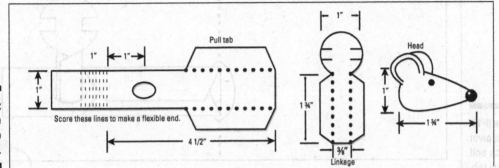

Figure 8-13:
Copy the pieces onto card.

4. **Score along the dotted and dashed lines, cut out any holes with a sharp knife, and use scissors to cut the rest.**

5. **Complete the pull tab and linkage by folding the tabs over and gluing them down (see Figure 8-14).**

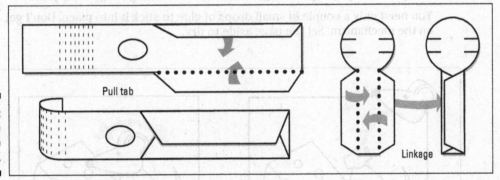

Figure 8-14:
Assemble the pull tab and linkage.

6. **Fit the linkage into place in the card.**

   From the back of the card, thread the two tabs of the linkage into place so that they stick out through the hole. Fold them down flat on the front of the card.

7. **Fit the pull tab over the linkage and glue the end of the pull tab to the card.**

   The pull-end of the pull tab should be sticking out though the hole in the center of the card ever so slightly. Figure 8-15 shows how the parts join.

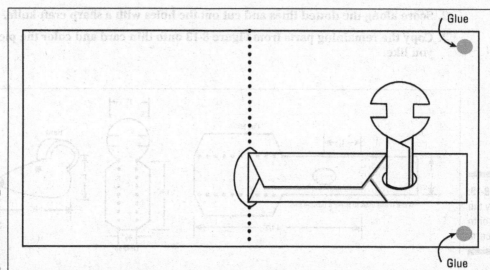

Figure 8-15:
Fit the pivot piece and the pull tab.

8. **On the front of the card, glue the mouse's head onto the tabs of the linkage.**

   Make sure you don't get any glue where it shouldn't be and that the head is free to move. Figure 8-16 shows the result.

9. **Complete the page by folding the card around and gluing it into place.**

   You need only a couple of small drops of glue to stick it into place. Don't get any glue on the mechanism. Set the page aside to dry.

Figure 8-16:
Glue the head into place on the front of the page.

Pop-out jump: Page three, the mouse is happy

In the final page of the mouse's story, the mouse realizes what he has found and jumps for joy. The mechanism in this section, which combines a pull tab with a pop-up, is good for making things jump. It works either across the page or up and down. A pull tab at the bottom of the page is connected by paper levers to a cutout of the happy mouse. Pull the tab, and a lever lifts the mouse so that he leaps, popping out of the page. This mechanism would be perfect for a jumping frog, a cat pouncing on a mouse or, of course, a mouse jumping for joy.

Follow these instructions to make the last page of the mouse book:

1. **Copy the template from Figure 8-17 onto a sheet of white card.**

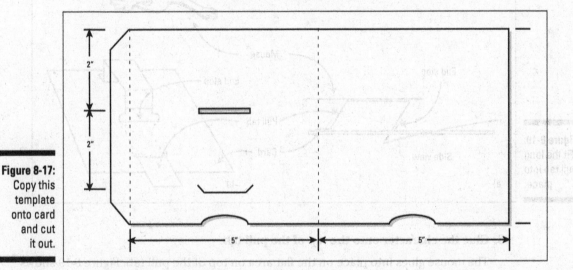

Figure 8-17:
Copy this template onto card and cut it out.

2. **Score along the dashed lines, carefully use a sharp knife to cut out the holes, and cut out the card using your scissors.**

3. **Copy the three other parts from Figure 8-18 onto a sheet of white card.**

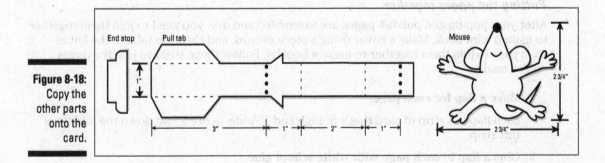

Figure 8-18:
Copy the other parts onto the card.

4. **Score along the dotted and dashed lines, color the parts as you like, and carefully cut them out.**

5. **Thread the long pull tab into place and glue it to the card.**

   Fold in the tabs on the side of the long tab and glue them down to strengthen the pull tab. Figure 8-19a shows a side view of how the pull tab fits into place, and Figure 8-19b gives the top view.

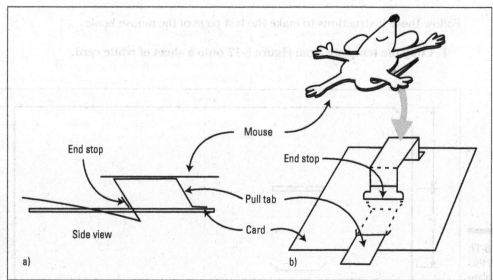

Figure 8-19:
Fit the long pull tab into place.

6. **Glue the character onto the top of the pull tab.**

   The mouse glues into place on the flat area on top of the pull tab. Figure 8-19 shows where it fits.

7. **Complete the page by folding the back around and gluing it down.**

   Again, you need only a couple of drops of glue to hold the back in place. Make sure you don't get any glue on the mechanism, and set the page aside to dry.

Putting the pages together

After your pop-up and pull-tab pages are assembled and dry, you need to join them together to make a mini-book. Make a cover using a piece of card, and then use tabs to the left of each page to join them together to make a booklet. Follow these steps to join the pages you've made:

1. **Make a flap for each page.**

   Each flap is a strip of card that's 5" high and 1" wide. Score a fold down the middle of this strip.

2. **Glue a flap to each page with white school glue.**

For each page, glue the strip to the left-hand edge of the card. Line up the crease line with the edge of the card and glue the strip to the back of the card so that it's out of the way.

3. **Glue the flaps to the adjoining pages and to the cover, as Figure 8-20 shows.**

Use the three flaps to join the three pages together and to glue the cover into place. Each flap attaches to the back of the page that comes before it.

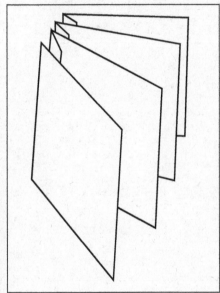

Figure 8-20:
Join the pages to make a booklet.

Part III

Paper Sculpture and Animation: Adding Some 3D Life to Paper

The 5th Wave   By Rich Tennant

"Well, Mr. Bridges, it appears that working on your paper animations for hours on end certainly DOES have some side effects."

In this part . . .

In this part, you get to bring your designs into the real world by transforming flat paper into 3D models. Here, I introduce you to paper sculpture. I also explain paper animations, or *automata*, which are paper machines that use paper mechanisms to come to life. Through a whole range of practical projects, I show you how you can use mechanisms — such as levers, linkages, and cams — to make your paper characters move in a realistic way.

Chapter 9

Paper Sculpture: 3D Art from Paper or Card

. . . .

In This Chapter

▶ Understanding paper sculpture basics

▶ Creating in three dimensions

▶ Making mounted or framed sculptures

▶ Folding origami creations

. . . .

When you think of sculpture, you probably think of clay, marble, wood, bronze, or stone. Paper probably isn't at the top of your list, but don't feel limited with paper. Although people use paper as a flat surface most of the time, with the art going on the paper, the paper *is* the art with paper sculpture. You make the sculpture by curving or folding the surface into a 3D form and using the texture and color of the paper to make interesting and artistic shapes. With just with some clever cuts or folds and a little imagination, you can make some fabulous paper art.

Are you excited about taking a stab at what sculptures you can whip up with your paper? If so, this chapter provides you with a quick overview of the characteristics of paper sculptures and outlines a few projects you can try. I present 3D projects you can cut and assemble, tell you how to score paper so you can create creases that curve, and show you how origami lets you sculpt from a single square sheet of paper.

Identifying Key Characteristics of Paper Sculpture

Paper sculpture is the art of making beautiful 3D objects from flat sheets of paper. Characteristics of paper sculpture include the following:

✔ Paper sculptures are made from sheets of paper and card, often cut into shape and then glued together.

✔ Paper sculptures use curves and creases to make flat sheets of paper become 3D.

✔ Paper sculptures can use a variety of different types of paper and card within the same sculpture.

When making paper sculptures, you have many options. However, you may want to consider the following techniques to give your card the wow factor:

✔ **Curves and creases:** You can use them to stiffen paper and to make it into a 3D shape. Curved creases especially can make interesting 3D surfaces.

✔ **Cuts with a craft knife:** You can make very intricate cuts with a craft knife. These cuts let you add detail and pattern to your sculpture.

✔ **Origami:** Origami is the art of folding a single square sheet of paper without any cutting or gluing.

This chapter looks more closely at how you can fold, crease, and cut paper into incredible paper sculptures.

Creating a Freestanding Paper Sculpture

For centuries, artists, hobbyists, and children have been making paper sculptures. From the kid slicing up a cereal box to build a model battleship or a town for the Lone Ranger to the artist modeling endangered animals or Czechoslovakian castles, a lot of people have fallen in love with paper sculpture. Search online for "paper models" or "papercraft," and you'll find hundreds of free model templates you can download, print, and assemble. A lot of the templates are from fellow hobbyists, but even companies such as Yamaha Motor (www.yamaha-motor.co.jp/global/entertainment/papercraft) and Canon (www.canon.com/c-park) are getting in on the action.

Part of the fun of paper sculpture, though, is drawing your own templates and designing new models. In this section, I give you some tips on designing in 3D and introduce a simple water lily sculpture.

Working in 3D

The challenge of paper sculpture is figuring out how to turn a flat sheet of paper into something that has depth, height, and width. You generally can't mold, chisel, or carve paper the way you do with other sculpting materials, so you have to score, fold, cut, curl, layer, and glue the paper to make your project.

As you design and build your paper sculpture, follow these tips:

✔ **Choose how you want to design your sculptures.** You basically have two ways:

  • Draw them out on paper in your notebook and plan all the details of the model before you start building.

  • Just start cutting and sticking.

Both techniques work well. I sketch when I know what I'm designing. When I'm just trying to be creative, I get out the scissors and snip, snip, snip.

TIP

Color, white, what's right?

Sometimes models look great just in white, and some projects need color — so how do you decide? Your final decision depends on your personal preference. There's no right or wrong answer. These guidelines can help you make your decision:

✔ For a more abstract effect, use white or go *monochromatic* (use only one color). Don't forget, though, that if you have a flat model with no color, it'll be very hard to see what's going on. A white-only paper sculpture works best with lots of 3D shape. The shadows and highlights really bring out the depth of the model.

✔ If your model is aimed at being as real-to-life as possible, then it will look better in full color. Scale models of buildings or vehicles look best if they accurately represent both the shape and color of the subject.

So what's the best way to add color to your model? You can either use precolored materials or color the materials with paint or pen before or after you've completed your model. Spray paint works well for sculptures, but you have to use it in a well-ventilated area. Chapter 4 discusses some general coloring methods.

✔ **Keep everything clean.** When you're making your sculpture, make sure your hands and work surface are clean and that you don't get any excess glue on your work. This tip is especially important for paper sculptures because people can view these works from any angle.

✔ **Use the appropriate paper.** You need to use fairly heavy paper for paper sculptures so that your finished piece doesn't flop over. Look for paper that is at least 150 g/m^2 or 90 pounds. (See Chapter 2 for info on paper weight.)

✔ **Add texture to your paper before you add it to your sculpture.** Press the flat of a scissor blade or the handle of your craft knife into the back of your paper to *emboss* it (raise it slightly). Or check out your craft store for proper embossing tools.

✔ **Experiment with the paper to get different effects.** For example, you can run a long strip of paper over the edge of a pair of scissors to make a curly strip.

Project 9-1: Water Lily Sculpture

This paper water lily sculpture is as beautiful as it is simple. It involves cutting, scoring, folding, and layering paper before you glue it to a lilypad base. You can make the baseboard from a single sheet of card stock. You glue two rows of petals into place on top of the baseboard, along with some paper leaves. The finished result is an elegant water lily with a layered look that defies the simplicity of its construction.

Tools and Materials

2 to 3 sheets of thin white card

Ruler

Pencil and eraser

Scissors or a sharp craft knife

Cutting mat

White school glue and glue spreader

1. **Copy the templates from Figure 9-1 onto a sheet of card and cut them out.**

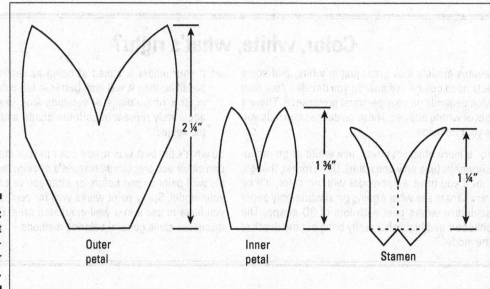

Figure 9-1:
Cut out these templates for the flowers.

Outer petal — 2 ¼"

Inner petal — 1 ⅜"

Stamen — 1 ¼"

Three parts make up the flower: the large outer petals, the small inner petals, and the stamen. Copy the templates as accurately as possible. Then cut them out to create patterns that you'll trace around in the next step.

2. **Draw around the petal and stamen patterns you created in Step 1.**

   The final flower has six of the large outer petals and six of the small inner petals. Draw around each petal pattern six times, each time carefully lining up the pattern with the outline you've just drawn. Erase part of the lines where the petals touch each other to make them dashed — these are score lines.

   Trace around the stamen pattern three times, creating three separate pieces.

3. **Draw a tab on each of the petal parts and stamen as well as a tab to close the petal shapes.**

   Look at the petals in Figure 9-2. Draw a small tab on the base of each petal as shown and also draw a tab to close the petals.

4. **Score along the dotted lines and cut out the petal and stamen parts.**

   Cut in toward the center of the cuts to get the best quality cuts. If you cut outward from the corners, the card tends to twist, leaving unwanted kinks in your work.

5. **Glue the petals together and glue them to the center of a sheet of card.**

   Glue down the tab that closes each set of petals, creating two rings of petals (see Figure 9-3). The two sets of petals fit one inside the other. Fold the tabs from the outer petals outward and those from the inner petals inward; glue them to a sheet of card (your baseboard).

Figure 9-2:
Add tabs to
the petals.

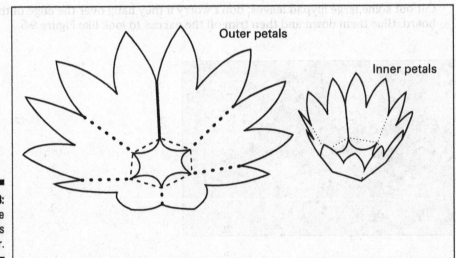

Outer petals

Inner petals

Figure 9-3:
Glue the
petals
together.

6. Glue together the stamen parts and glue them into the center of the flower.

The stamen is made of three identical stamen pieces. Fold two of them in half and glue two halves together; then glue the third stamen piece into place so that it touches the other two stamen pieces (see Figure 9-4). Glue the finished stamen into the center of the flower.

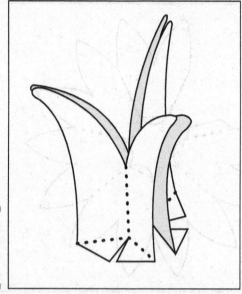

Figure 9-4:
Glue the
stamen
together.

7. Finish the model by adding two or three large leaves to the base piece of card stock.

Cut out some large lilypad leaves; don't worry if they hang over the edge of the base-board. Glue them down and then trim off the excess to look like Figure 9-5.

Figure 9-5:
Glue some
leaves into
place and
trim them
down to
size.

This sculpture works well as a white model, but it also looks good in color.

Shallow Sculptures: Limiting the Point of View

With paper, you can create sculptures that aren't very deep and that don't allow viewers to see all the way around them. Not only is this technique artistic, but it also saves you the trouble of having to design the back of your project. Some people glue their paper sculptures directly to a background, but you can also attach your sculpture to a deep picture frame that lets the pieces seem to float. In this section, I tell you how curved creases can add interest to these shallow sculptures, and I introduce a fun ladybug project.

Adding a little depth with curves and creases

One way paper engineers make 3D shapes is by creasing the paper. Most of the time the lines are straight, but by making your creases curved, you can make some interesting effects with your sculptures.

When you fold a curved score line, you end up with a curved edge, as you'd expect. You also get two curved surfaces, one on either side of the edge:

- ✔ **Convex face:** The outside of the curve, like the surface of a ball
- ✔ **Concave face:** The inside of the curve, like the inside of a bowl

As the light shines on those curved surfaces, it can create some interesting shadows.

You can use curved creases in freestanding sculptures, too (see the earlier "Creating a Freestanding Sculpture" section), but these creases are especially effective in shallow, mounted sculptures. Curved creases can't fold all the way down like straight creases do, so you can use them to add a little depth to your project without worrying about what they look like from the back. These types of projects can be especially elegant; the curves and smooth lines contrast with the straight lines of normal paper engineering.

When creating curved creases, make sure you score the crease line before folding. Scoring makes the crease go where you want it. Curved creases tend to wander off line, and a score line prevents this.

When you're scoring curved lines, make sure you have a nice, flowing curve. Sharp changes of direction make it difficult to fold the sculpture later on. Also, don't curve around more than half a circle.

Project 9-2: Ladybug in the Grass

Here's a simple, shallow sculpture project that uses curved creases. A 3D picture sits within a deep frame, using shadow and shape to make a delightful scene. Because the blades of grass aren't attached to the background, they seem to float, and you get some cool shadow effects that change if you move from side to side as you look at the sculpture. A ladybug finishes the project with a spot of color.

Look at Figure 9-6 to see the finished project. This simple scene is of grass and a ladybug.

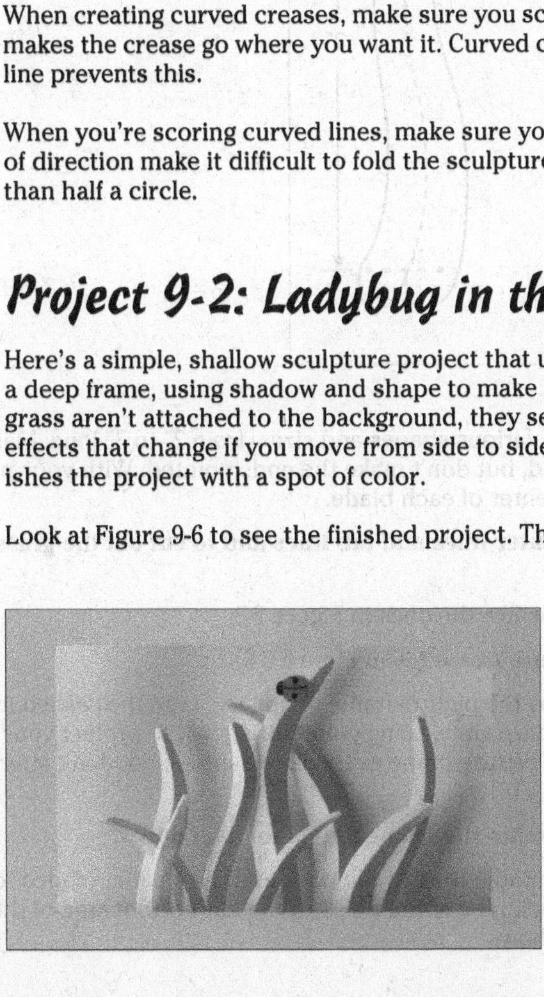

Figure 9-6: Curved creases add depth to the sculpture.

Tools and Materials

3 sheets of thin white card

Pencil and eraser

Scissors for scoring and cutting

Ruler

Sharp craft knife

Cutting mat

White school glue and glue spreader

Scrap of red card or a red felt-tipped pen

Fine black felt-tipped pen

1. **Draw 9 to 12 blades of grass on your white card, modeling them after Figure 9-7.**

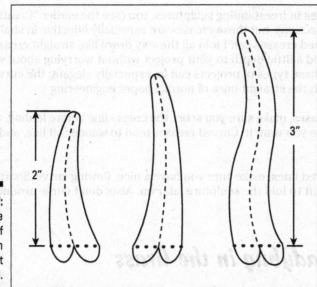

Figure 9-7:
Draw the
blades of
grass on
a sheet
of card.

The grass blades should be various shapes and sizes, from 2" to 3" long. Make them taper slightly toward the end, but don't make the ends pointed. With your pencil, mark out the crease line up the center of each blade.

2. **Use scissors to score the center lines and tab lines and to cut out the grass blades; fold along the score lines.**

The blades of grass now look like the ones in Figure 9-8.

3. **Make the parts for the picture frame (as in Figure 9-9).**

Using a ruler and pencil, copy the picture frame template. Score the dashed lines and cut out the hole with your sharp knife, using your cutting mat to protect your work surface. Fold up the back of the picture frame as the figure shows, but don't glue the parts together yet.

4. **Arrange the grass blades within the frame and glue them down.**

Put the taller blades in the middle toward the back and the smaller blades toward the sides and front. Glue the small tabs of the grass to the flat bottom area of the picture frame back, as Figure 9-10 shows.

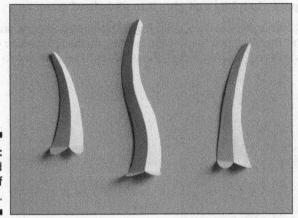

Figure 9-8:
Completed
blades of
grass.

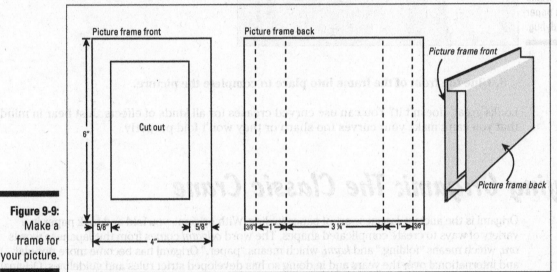

Picture frame front

Picture frame back

Picture frame front

Cut out

6"

Picture frame back

5/8"   5/8"

4"

3/8"   1"   3 ¼"   1"   3/8"

Figure 9-9:
Make a
frame for
your picture.

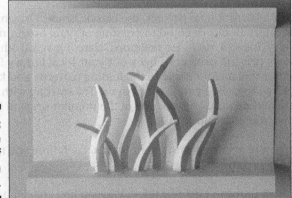

Figure 9-10:
Arrange the
blades of
grass within
the frame.

5. **Draw and cut out a red paper ladybug and glue it to a blade of grass.**

   Carefully draw the ladybug onto a piece of card, color it in using felt-tipped pens, and then cut it out with your scissors. Use the black pen to draw the ladybug on the red card, or draw it on white card and color it in with a red pen. Figure 9-11 shows the ladybug attached to the grass.

Figure 9-11: Make a paper ladybug.

6. **Glue the front of the frame into place to complete the picture.**

Looks great, doesn't it? You can use curved creases for all kinds of effects. Just bear in mind that you can't make your curves too sharp or they won't fold properly.

Trying Origami: The Classic Crane

Origami is the ancient Japanese art of paper folding. With origami, you fold and tuck paper in a variety of ways to create complicated shapes. The word *origami* comes from the Japanese words *oru*, which means "folding," and *kami*, which means "paper." Origami has become more popular and international over the years and in doing so has developed strict rules and guidelines. Original origami from the Edo period in Japan (around 1600 CE) allowed different paper shapes and allowed artists to cut the paper. Modern origami uses only a single square of paper with no cuts.

In this section, I provide you with a fairly simple project, the classic crane. Origami is such a complex topic that you can find entire books devoted to creating origami boxes, monsters, geometric shapes, aircraft, jewelry, insects, or *T. rex* skeletons. Here, I just introduce you to the fine art. If you want to do more origami projects, check out your local library for a multitude of other origami books. After you master some of the folding patterns and know how to fold some origami bases, feel free to create your own designs. Try starting with someone else's design and changing some of the folds, or make one of the popular origami bases, add some random folds, and see what you come up with.

When doing origami, make sure you're accurate with your creases. Each time you make a fold, you multiply the effects of any errors.

Use thin paper so that as you fold it, it doesn't get too thick. You can find special precut origami paper in craft, toy, and book shops. Origami paper is best, but if you can't get a hold of special origami paper or you can't wait to get started, you can use a piece of photocopy paper cut to size.

Project 9-3: Origami Crane

This crane project is pure origami, so a square of paper is all you need (that means you can put your scoring scissors away).

Tools and Materials

1 square of thin paper, approximately 8" x 8"

1. **Fold the paper in half diagonally and then fold it along the other diagonal; unfold the paper completely.**

   Fold corner to corner as in Figure 9-12. Then sharpen the crease by running your fingernail along the length of the crease.

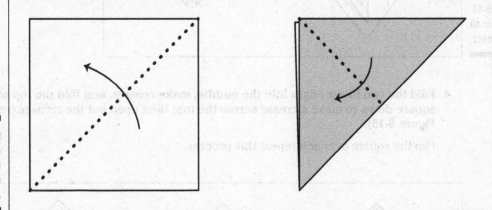

Figure 9-12:
Fold the paper in half on the diagonals.

2. **Fold the paper in half along the vertical and horizontal lines as in Figure 9-13.**

   Open the paper out; you should now have four crease lines on your paper.

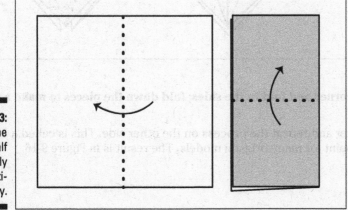

Figure 9-13:
Fold the paper in half horizontally and vertically.

3. **Bring all four corners together and fold the paper flat.**

   You now have a square half the size of the original square. See Figure 9-14.

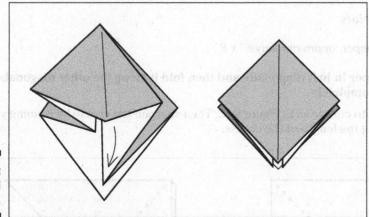

Figure 9-14:
Fold in all
the corners.

4. **Fold the two lower edges into the middle, make creases, and fold the top of the square down to make a crease across the top; then open out the creases (refer to Figure 9-15).**

   Flip the square over and repeat this process.

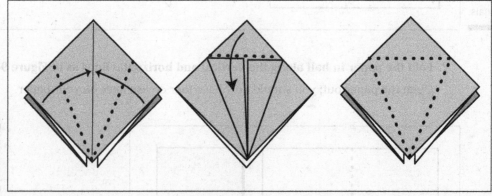

Figure 9-15:
Make these
creases.

5. **Lift the bottom corner and fold in the sides; fold down the pieces to make a tall, thin diamond shape.**

   Flip the paper over and repeat the process on the other side. This is called a *bird base*. It's the starting point for many origami models. The result is in Figure 9-16.

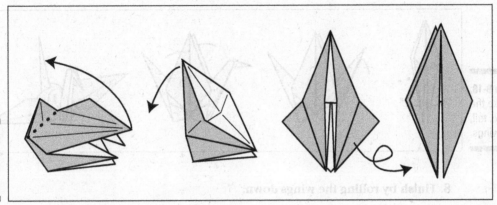

Figure 9-16:
Complete
the bird
base.

6. **Fold in the sides as Figure 9-17 shows.**

   Then flip the paper over and repeat the process. Nearly done!

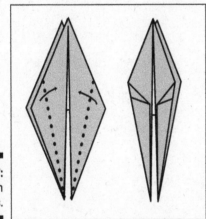

Figure 9-17:
Fold in
the sides.

7. **Fold the two long pieces up and make the head and tail as in Figure 9-18.**

   Notice that the parts you fold up go inside the two parts that will be the wings. First simply crease the long pieces along the dotted lines. Then open the sides slightly and bring the long pieces up, reversing the direction of the folds. Press flat.

   Pick one of the pieces to be the head and fold it down to make a beak. Open out the neck slightly, fold the head down inside the neck, and then flatten the neck again.

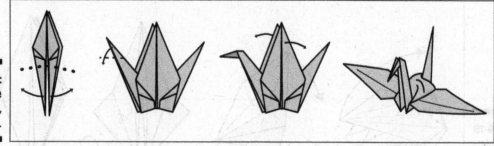

8. Finish by rolling the wings down.

Gently curve the wings by running them between your fingers and thumb. Figure 9-18 shows the completed model.

That's the completed origami crane. Try making cranes of different sizes and colors. Use patterned paper to make crane models — paper with a Japanese theme works especially well.

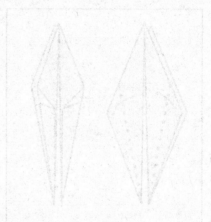

Chapter 10

Lights, Cams, Action! Having Fun with Paper Animations

. . . .

In This Chapter

▶ Getting a feel for simple cams

▶ Eyeing cam variations

. . . .

*E*lectronic gadgets can be a lot of fun, but if you crack open their cases to see how they work, you often end up staring at a collection of chips and wires. The insides would be a little more exciting if you could watch the electricity flow, but electronics are pretty much a closed set. If you really want to see some movement and watch how machines work (and skip the risk of getting shocked), look no further than paper animations.

Paper animations are *automata,* a technical term that means they're machines that use levers, cranks, linkages, and so on to come to life. For example, the animation may be a model of a surfing spider or a row of chickens pecking the dust in search of some crumbs of food. In a typical automaton, the *mechanism,* the part that does the work, is concealed within the base, and the action takes place on top of the base. However, I like to have an open base in my models so that anyone who's interested can see how it all works.

Simple but effective, the cam is at the heart of many paper animation models. A *cam* is like a wheel that turns on a shaft; the wheel is usually off-center or a shape other than a circle so that as the cam turns, its changing surface pushes a lever or pushrod up and down. Cams can be any shape, from the simplest oval cam to the most complex up-and-down wavy edge. In this chapter, I introduce the basic cam and then show you how to use multiple cams or irregularly shaped cams to tell a whole variety of stories.

Creating a Simple Cam Model

If you want to take a stab at working with cam models, starting with a simple one is the way to go. This section gives you a quick overview of cam models and presents a cam project you may want to try.

The look and feel of a simple cam model

Working with a simple cam model can be fun if you're the type of person who likes to see how things work. With a cam, you can make things move up and down, but that's not the end of the story. By choosing the shape of the cam, you can choose how quickly and by how much things move. Want something to move quickly? Choose a cam with a crinkly edge. Smoothly? Give your cam a gently curved edge. Then, by linking your up-and-down motion to a couple of levers or linkages, you can make an arm wave, eyes roll, or a pirate pop his head out of a barrel.

A cam model uses three basic components:

✔ **The cam:** That's the wheel-like part that turns and does the work.

✔ **The camshaft:** The camshaft is the part that the cam is attached to. Typically, the camshaft fits through holes in the model base and is free to turn.

✔ **The cam follower:** This is the part that actually touches the cam. The cam follower transfers the movement from the cam to the paper animation.

Figure 10-1 shows a typical cam model.

Figure 10-1:
Turn the handle to see the action.

A vital part of most mechanisms is the linkage. The *linkage* joins parts together, transferring motion from one part of the model to another. In a cam model, the cam rotates, which in turn moves the cam follower. For the cam follower to do anything useful, it then needs a linkage to connect it to another part of the model.

In a paper animation, if you need only to pull, then a simple strip of paper will do. But just as you can't push a piece of string, pushing on a strip of paper does nothing. Most of the linkages I use are made from triangular tubes of paper. These are surprisingly strong and stiff. Perfect for the job in hand! (For more on creating triangular tubes for strength, check out Chapter 11.)

Project 10-1: Octopus Action

The Octopus Action project is a simple paper animation that uses a single, regular cam to control the action. Turn the handle on the side of the box, and the octopus floats up and down, waving his tentacles behind him.

Tools and Materials

2 sheets of thin white card	Cutting mat
1 sheet of flexible white paper	Drawing compass
Ruler	Scissors
Pencil and eraser	A penny
Sharp craft knife	White school glue and glue spreader

1. **Copy the box parts templates from Figure 10-2 onto your card.**

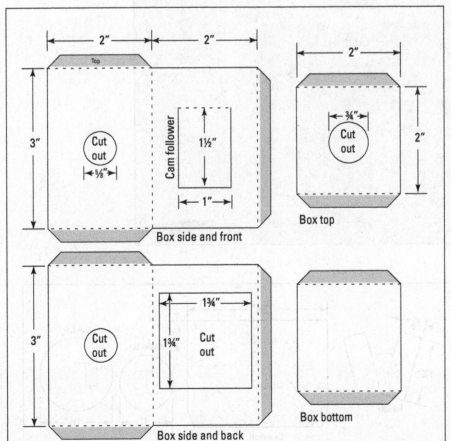

Figure 10-2: Copy these parts onto white card.

2. **Score the dashed lines of the parts and then cut them out.**

   Fold the creases before you start assembly to make sure that they're nice and sharp. Use a sharp knife to cut out the holes in the box parts.

3. **Glue the sides of the box to the front and back; then glue on the top and bottom.**

   Notice that the top piece has a hole in it. Make sure the top is glued to the flap that says *top* on it. The result looks like Figure 10-3.

4. **Wrap a penny in paper and glue it to the back of the flap on the front of the box.**

   This flap is the cam follower. The penny gives it some weight so it's always touching the cam.

5. **Copy the mechanism parts from the template in Figure 10-4 onto white card, score along the dashed lines, and cut out the pieces.**

6. **Roll around and glue the camshaft together.**

   The camshaft is a square tube. Fold the piece around on itself and glue the flap down.

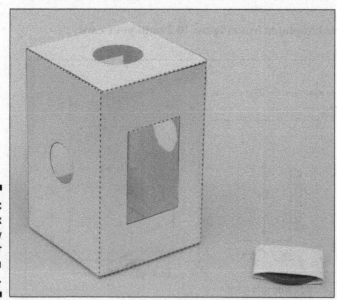

Figure 10-3:
The box and penny weight for the cam follower.

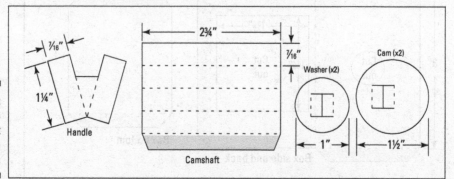

Figure 10-4:
Copy the camshaft parts on to thin card.

7. Glue the two halves of the cam together and then glue them onto the middle of the camshaft.

The two parts of the cam are identical. Glue them back-to-back but don't get any glue on the four flaps yet. When they're dry, slide the cam onto the camshaft and glue the four flaps down. Figure 10-5 shows the completed camshaft.

8. Fit the camshaft into the box and secure it with the washers.

Do this with the box upside down so that the cam follower falls out of the way. You need to do this step from the back of the box. After the camshaft is in place, slide on the washers and glue them into place on the camshaft (don't glue them to the box). Leave enough room for the handle. Don't put them on too tight, and make sure that the camshaft can turn freely in the box.

9. Glue the simple handle into place on the end of the camshaft.

This is a really easy to make handle. Just fold it up and glue the two ends directly to the camshaft (see Figure 10-6). (For a more-complex crank handle, see Chapter 11.)

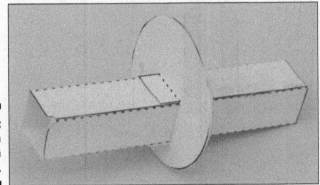

Figure 10-5:
Glue the cam to the camshaft.

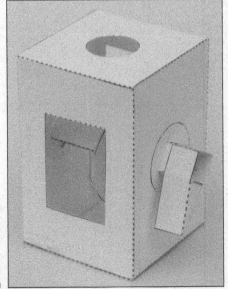

Figure 10-6:
Fit the handle to the camshaft.

10. **Mark out the templates from Figure 10-7 onto paper and card.**

    These are the parts that make up the octopus. The tentacles are made from paper rather than card to make them flexible.

11. **Fold the long flaps on the body center into place and glue them down.**

    See Figure 10-8. Folding these flaps in makes the center pushrod strong and rigid.

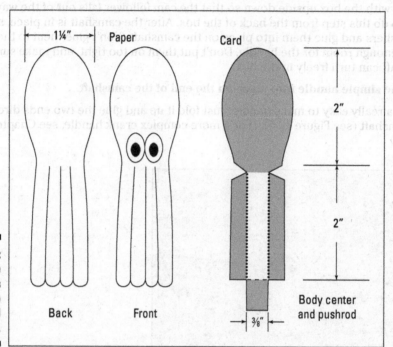

Figure 10-7: Copy the octopus parts onto paper and card.

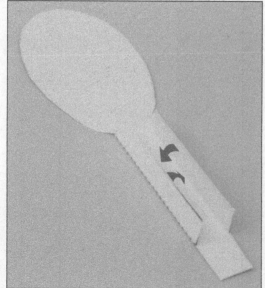

Figure 10-8: Make the octopus center.

12. **Glue the front and back of the octopus into place on the body center, as Figure 10-9 shows.**

    Make sure you only glue the body; the tentacles should be free to move.

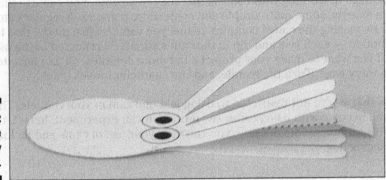

Figure 10-9: Glue the body together.

13. **Thread the pushrod down through the hole in the top of the box and glue it to the cam follower.**

    Glue the flap at the end of the pushrod to the cam follower (the flap with the penny wrapped in paper).

14. **Finish the model by gluing the tentacles to the box top.**

    Try to space them evenly around the hole in the box top. Give the tentacles a gentle curve before you join them to the box top.

Figure 10-10 shows the finished model. Turn the handle and watch the octopus bob up and down. You can add to the model by using colored card or by adding color with pens or paint. Why not finish it off with some tassels of seaweed or drawings of fish on the box?

Figure 10-10: Octopus Action.

Story Variations: Using Irregular and Multiple Cams

One great advantage to working with cams is that they're flexible. You can use them in all kinds of movements, some quite simple and some more complex. Irregular cams have uneven edges. By making the cam a complex shape, you can design a model that has a more complicated motion — each rise and dip in the cam's surface is reflected in the movement of the model. If you want to make your project a tad more complex, all you have to do is give the cam a wavy edge. Turn the handle, and the character moves quickly.

What's great is that you're not restricted to using just one cam in your models. The more comfortable you become with using cams, the more you can experiment. In fact, the more the merrier. This section points out how you can vary your use of cams and includes a fun project of a dancing dog.

Varying the amount and type of movement

You can use your cams to create all sorts of complex movements. Here are some ways changing the cam can change the way your paper animation moves:

- **Off-center circle:** A cam that's an off-center circle produces a smooth back-and-forth motion in the cam follower. It's perfect for powering a waving hand or a nodding head.

- **Size:** By changing the size of the cam, you can change how much the cam follower moves. The bigger the cam, the more space for cam-follower movement.

- **Wavy edges:** The more waves at the edge of the cam, the faster the movement. A wavy edge moves your model fast but with a nice, smooth action. Wavy edges are ideal for a model with some running legs.

- **Straight edges:** A cam made of straight edges, like the edge of a saw, makes the cam follower move in jerky, sharp steps. These edges are perfect if you're making a robot model and want jerky, robotic movements. (*Note:* Besides referring to a paper animation, *automaton* is also another word for a robot, so making an automaton paper animation is doubly cool.)

- **Irregular shapes:** If you want to tell a story with your cam, you need an irregular shape. You can use irregular shapes for all kinds of motion. For example, a model in which a wolf howls at the moon can use an irregular cam to make the howl movements different lengths.

Adding another cam to the camshaft makes your paper animation a multicam project. A second cam, connected to the same shaft, works in exactly the same way as the first. Each cam uses its own cam follower, and as the camshaft turns, the separate cams describe their own unique motions. Some complex wooden and metal automata have tons of cams all attached to the same shaft, each controlling a particular part of the model.

Imagine you have a moose model that nods because of an off-center circle cam (like the one in Chapter 11), but on his back you want to add a little bird hopping up and down. Nodding may be slow and thoughtful, but a bird hopping should be quick and lively. How can you achieve this effect? Simple: Just add another cam, perhaps with a wavy edge, to the camshaft. Connect another cam follower to a paper bird, and your model is complete.

As you use multiple cams and experiment with cam shapes, look for ways to vary the story. Even if the cams are the same size and shape, you can rotate one cam slightly so that different parts of the animation rise and fall at different times.

Project 10-2: The Dancing Dog

You can create quite complex movements by using irregular cams. Suppose you want a model in which an animal does a crazy dance. An irregular cam connected to each foot is perfect for the job.

The Dancing Dog (Figure 10-11) is a great example of a project that uses irregular cams. The two cams control the front and back of the dog separately. As you turn the handle, the front of the dog jumps up twice; then the back of the dog jumps up twice. The process repeats itself over and over as you turn the handle, so the dog dances!

Figure 10-11: The Dancing Dog.

Tools and Materials

2 sheets of thin card

Ruler

Pencil and eraser

Sharp craft knife

Cutting mat

Drawing compass

Scissors

Two pennies

White school glue and glue spreader

Tweezers (optional)

1. **Copy the box parts templates and cut out the parts.**

   Copy the templates in Figure 10-12 onto a sheet of card. You need two box ends. Score along the dotted lines, cut out the holes, and then cut out all the parts.

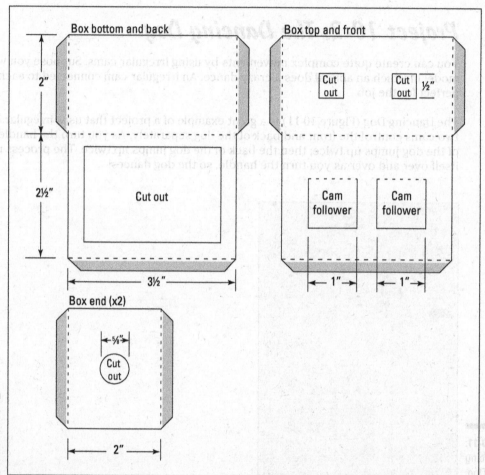

Figure 10-12: Copy the box parts onto card.

2. **Glue the box together.**

   Glue the two large parts together first and then glue on the two ends. Figure 10-13 shows the completed box.

3. **Draw and cut out the parts of the mechanism.**

   Copy the templates from Figure 10-14 onto thin card. Score the dashed lines, cut the holes with a sharp knife, and then cut out the parts.

4. **Glue together the two pairs of cams.**

   The four cam parts are identical. Glue pairs of cam pieces back-to-back to make two identical cams, leaving the tabs free. The extra thickness is for strength.

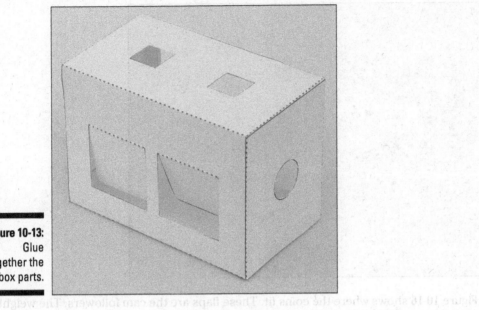

Figure 10-13:
Glue together the box parts.

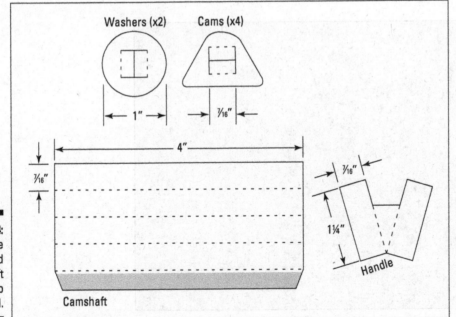

Figure 10-14:
Copy the cam and camshaft parts onto thin card.

5. **Fold around and glue the camshaft, and glue on the cams.**

   Fold around and glue the camshaft. Slide the two cams into place on the camshaft. Notice in Figure 10-15 that one is pointing up and the other is pointing down.

6. **Glue flaps of paper around two pennies; then glue them to the back of the flaps in the front of the box.**

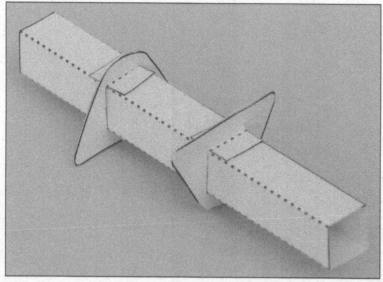

Figure 10-15:
Assemble
the
camshaft.

Figure 10-16 shows where the coins fit. These flaps are the cam followers. The weight of the coin ensures that the cam follower stays close to the cam.

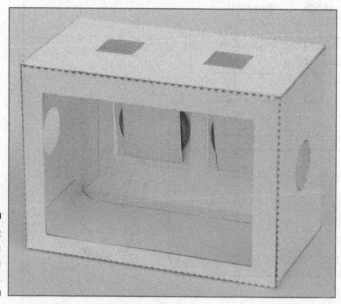

Figure 10-16:
Add coins
to the cam
followers.

7. Fit the camshaft into the box.

Turn the box upside down so that the cam followers fall out of the way. From the back of the box, carefully fit the camshaft into place as Figure 10-17 shows: Fix it into place by gluing the washers to the camshaft (not to the box). Make sure that the camshaft is free to turn in the box and that you leave enough room for the handle.

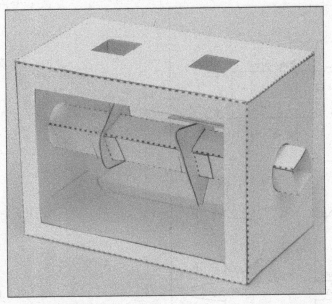

Figure 10-17:
Fit the cam-
shaft into
place.

8. Glue the simple handle to the end of the camshaft.

Figure 10-18 shows how the handle fits into place. (Check out the next chapter for a more-advanced handle.)

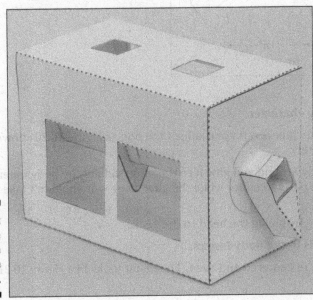

Figure 10-18:
Add the
handle
to the
camshaft.

9. Copy the dog templates from Figure 10-19 onto thin card and cut out the parts.

This is the last of the templates for this project. You need two pushrods and two body inners. Score the dashed lines and carefully cut out the parts.

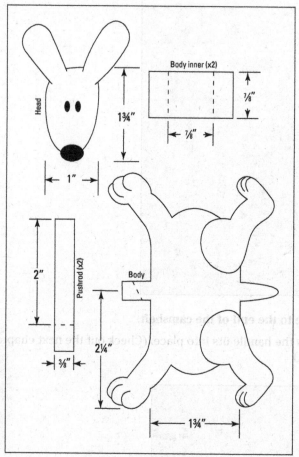

Body inner (x2)

⅛"

⅛"

Head

1¾"

1"

2"

Pushrod (x2)

⅜"

Body

2¼"

1¾"

Figure 10-19:
Copy the dog templates onto thin card.

10. Glue together the dog character.

1. Glue the two body inners onto one side of the dog as Figure 10-20 shows. Let the glue dry completely.

2. Fold the dog body around and glue it to the other side of the body inners. You need to hold the parts together while the glue dries — it shouldn't take more than a minute.

3. Finish off the dog by gluing the head to the neck.

11. Glue the two pushrods to the body inners.

Try to make sure they're centered and even. The result looks like Figure 10-21.

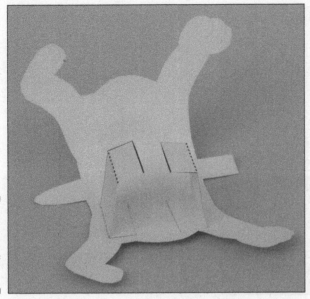

Figure 10-20:
Glue together the parts of the dog.

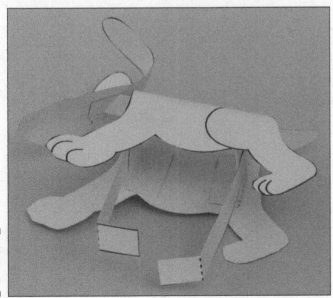

Figure 10-21:
Glue on the pushrods.

12. Thread the pushrods down through the holes in the top of the box and glue the ends to the cam followers.

You may find a set of tweezers handy here for clamping each tab to its cam follower. Figure 10-22 shows the end result. Let the glue dry completely before trying out your creation. After the glue is dry, turn the handle to see your dog dance.

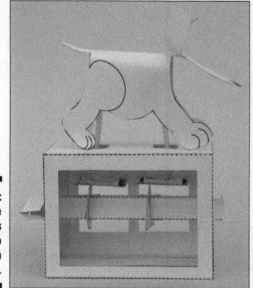

Figure 10-22:
The pushrods attach to the cam followers.

Chapter 11

Getting Past the Limitations of Paper in Your Paper Animations

. . . .

In This Chapter

▶ Adding weight to your models

▶ Redesigning the handle

▶ Making strong shapes

. . . .

If you hang out in art circles long enough, you may hear people talk about the "purity" of the art form. In other words, people want to know what kinds of materials are allowed before you stop being a paper engineer and start falling into the murky world of "mixed media artist." A while back, a forum on my Web site (www.flying-pig.co.uk) had a discussion about how pure paper models should be. I was criticized for not being pure, on my own forum! The cheek of it! The lively debate ended with people agreeing to differ.

Although you have many options when you're working with paper models, building with paper does have some limitations. Paper isn't the stongest material, so you need to think carefully about how things fit together to make the strongest possible shape. Some mechanisms, which are easy to make in traditional automata materials (wood, leather, and brass), are virtually impossible in paper. You can't make springs from paper, and anything needing weight is hard. As you design models from paper, you need to think of ways around these problems.

Because of these limitations, some people introduce nonpaper elements into their designs to add strength or weight. For example, some paper-animation makers use cocktail sticks and lengths of thread to make parts of their models. Others add extra weights to models to make them move better. I personally don't use string or sticks in my models, but I often use coins as weights.

My philosophy is that you can use things that you may have in your pocket but nothing else. Working within these limits can be fun because it forces you to be creative when solving problems — and you get to feel more like an engineer. In this chapter, I show you how to get past some of the challenges of working with paper while staying true to the art of paper engineering. You discover how to use paper to build a better handle and strengthen your shapes, as well as how coins can add some needed weight to your mechanisms.

Change Will Do You Good: Using Coins for Weight

You can use coins anywhere you need a part to move under its own power. For instance, you can return a lever to position, pulling a tortoise's head back into its shell or lifting a penguin's wings. As you may have noticed in Chapter 10, coin weights are also useful if you're using a cam to drive the action. A *cam* is like an irregularly shaped wheel that you use to move parts in a model. A cam pushes the cam follower upward, but you rely on gravity to return the part to its original position. Adding weight to the cam follower helps ensure that the cam follower always rests against the cam.

You can't use white school glue to glue a coin to your model. It won't stick! To get around this problem without having to introduce a new special glue, wrap the coin in a strip of paper or a paper cross like the one in Figure 11-1. You can then glue this coin packet to your model using white school glue.

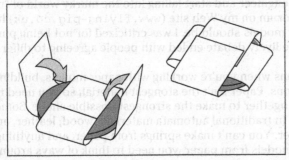

Figure 11-1:
Wrap your coin in paper.

Solving cardboard creep

Cardboard and paper are fun materials for designing moving models, but they do have their limitations. One of the problems that I've come across is something I call *cardboard creep*. The problem is that paper hinges tend to stay in the same position that you've left them in. If you have a model of a person doing push-ups, for example, you find that it works well if you leave it in the upright position (see Figure 11-2a), but if you leave the chap so that he's close to the ground (see Figure 11-2b), it doesn't work so well.

Here's how you can get around the problem of cardboard creep, ensuring that the model moves easily when you first start turning the handle:

1. **Make sure that there's a position in which you can leave your model so that it's at a full stretch.**

   For example, in a model with two birds that peck alternately, it's best if you can have a resting position in which both birds are upright.

2. **Add some coins for power.**

   If you're having problems with parts that don't return to their proper position (identified in Step 1), see whether you can add a coin or two to pull the part back to where it should be. (*Note:* If you can't add coins to return the model to a full stretch, you simply have to remember to stop turning the handle when the model is in the proper position.)

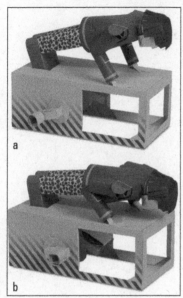

Project 11-1: The Nodding Moose

The Nodding Moose uses a cam and a cam follower that uses a coin as a weight. With this somewhat more-advanced project, the cam follower is a weighted, triangular tube rather than a simple flap of paper. Turn the handle on the box, and the paper moose nods his head rhythmically. Figure 11-3 shows the completed Nodding Moose model.

In the following sections, I break the model down, describe how to make each of the parts in turn, and then explain how to put all the parts together. (See Chapter 4 for techniques on marking your card, cutting, scoring, and gluing.)

Tools and Materials

5 pieces of thin card	*Drawing compass*
Ruler	*Protractor*
Pencil and eraser	*Scissors*
Sharp craft knife	*A penny*
Cutting mat	*White school glue and glue spreader*

Figure 11-3:
The com-
pleted
Nodding
Moose.

The box

The box is what houses the cam mechanism. Two round holes, one in each side, are ready for the camshaft. The box is open, front and back, so that the user can see how the model works. The top of the box has a hole for a pushrod to pass through so it can push the moose's head.

Follow these directions to make the box:

1. **Copy the box templates onto a sheet of card (see Figure 11-4).**

2. **Score the crease lines and cut out the holes.**

   Cut out the holes in the card using a sharp craft knife. Score the dashed fold lines with a pair of scissors.

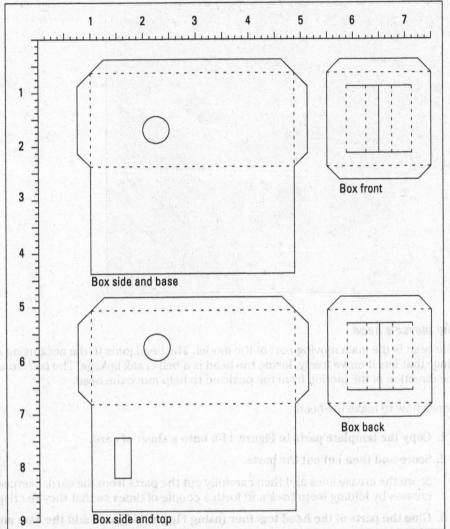

Figure 11-4:
Mark out
the parts of
the box onto
a sheet
of card.

3. Cut out the pieces with your scissors.

Cut as carefully and accurately as possible; the neater the cut, the better the model will be.

4. Glue together the pieces to complete the box.

After you complete the box, fold in the flaps at the front and back and glue them to the inside of the box (see Figure 11-5). This adds strength to the box and keeps the edges of the cutout at the front of the box neat.

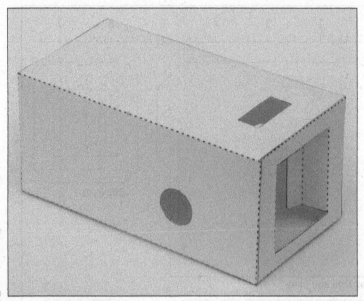

The moose's head

The head is the main moving part of the model. The head joins to the neck using a card hinge that lets it move freely. Inside the head is a bell crank linkage. The *bell crank* changes the direction of the motion from the pushrod to help move the head.

Here's how to make the head:

1. **Copy the template parts in Figure 11-6 onto a sheet of card.**

2. **Score and then cut out the parts.**

   Score the crease lines and then carefully cut the parts from the card. Exercise the creases by folding them back and forth a couple of times so that they're crisp and neat.

3. **Glue the parts of the head together (using Figure 11-7) and add the ears and antlers.**

   Gently curl the antlers upward.

4. **Assemble the bell crank and glue it inside the head (refer to Figure 11-8).**

   Don't get glue on the hinge flap, or it'll stiffen up!

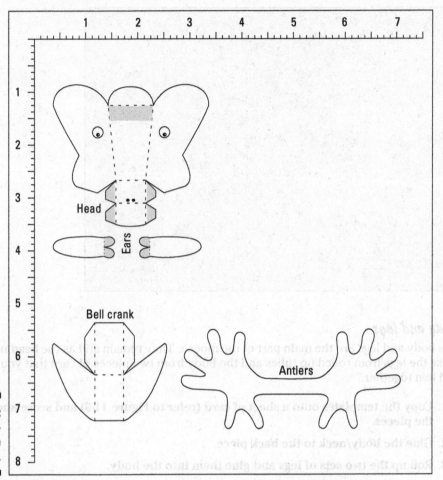

Head

Ears

Bell crank

Antlers

Figure 11-6:
The tem-
plate for the
head.

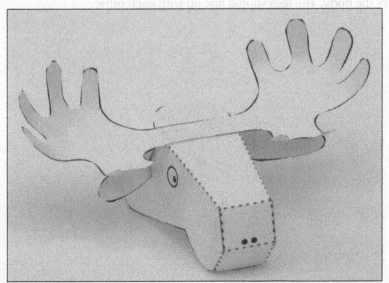

Figure 11-7:
Assemble
the head.

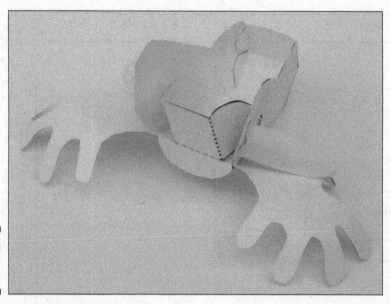

Figure 11-8:
Attach the
bell crank.

Body and legs

The body and legs are the main part of the moose. They remain still as the head nods. You make the legs from rolled up tubes and the body from two pieces of card that you fold over and join together.

1. **Copy the templates onto a sheet of card (refer to Figure 11-9) and score and cut out the pieces.**

2. **Glue the body/neck to the back piece.**

3. **Roll up the two sets of legs and glue them into the body.**

   Roll the legs as shown in Figure 11-10 and glue them into place so that they're touching the top of the body. The legs should line up with each other.

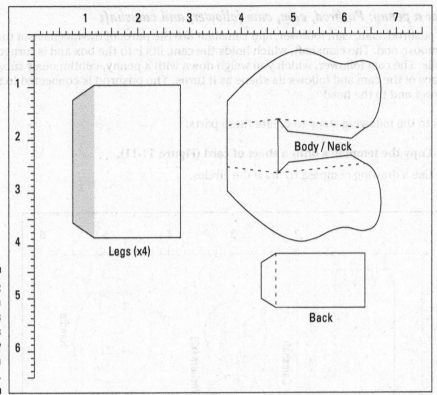

Figure 11-9:
Copy the templates for the legs and body onto thin card.

Legs (x4)

Body / Neck

Back

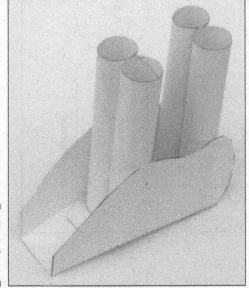

Figure 11-10:
Assemble the body and legs.

In for a penny: Pushrod, cam, cam follower, and camshaft

The pushrod, cam, cam follower, and camshaft are the parts of the mechanism that make the moose nod. The camshaft, which holds the cam, fits into the box and is turned by the handle. The cam follower, which you weigh down with a penny, continuously rubs over the surface of the cam and follows its shape as it turns. The pushrod is connected to the cam follower and to the head.

Stick to the following steps to create these parts:

1. **Copy the templates onto a sheet of card (Figure 11-11).**

   Use a drawing compass to draw the circles.

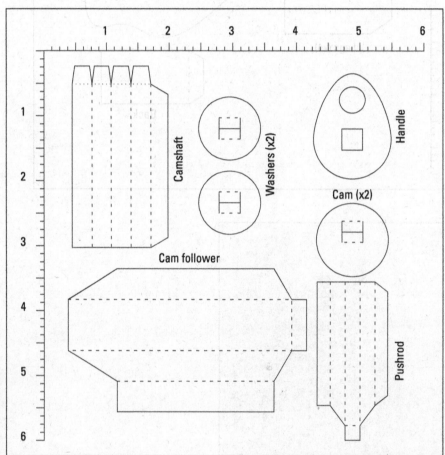

Figure 11-11:
The template for the cam parts.

2. Score and cut out the parts.

You have quite a few parts here, so make sure you don't get them mixed up. Carefully score the dashed lines and cut out the pieces.

3. Make the camshaft (as in Figure 11-12).

Fold the camshaft around and glue the wide flap down to make a square tube. Glue the two cam pieces together, avoiding the tabs, to make a double-thickness cam. Slide the cam onto the center of the camshaft, but don't glue it down for now.

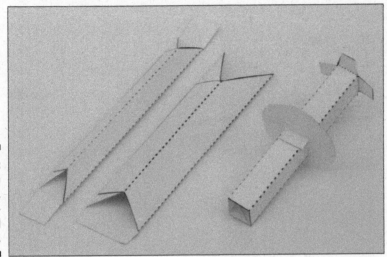

Figure 11-12:
Make the pushrod, cam follower, and camshaft.

4. Assemble the cam follower and pushrod (as in Figure 11-12).

Wrap a penny in a strip of paper or paper cross. Then glue the coin packet inside the cam follower, near the end without the tab. The coin adds weight to the cam follower and helps the head move. Fold around and glue the cam follower. Make the pushrod by folding the piece into a triangular tube and gluing it.

The tree

Using three parts, the stylized pine tree completes the model. It sits at the back of the box and adds a foresty theme.

1. Copy the template from Figure 11-13 onto a piece of card.

2. Score and cut out the pieces of the trunk using these steps:

1. Mark out one trunk length. Cut it out and draw around it. Use this template to mark out the other three sections of the trunk and a long tab. Add four small tabs to the bottom of the trunk sections.

2. Use a compass to draw two half-circles, one inside the other, for the lower branches. Mark a rough zigzag between the inner and outer circles. This represents the end of the tree branches. Repeat for the upper branches.

3. Carefully score the lines on the trunk and cut out all three pieces.

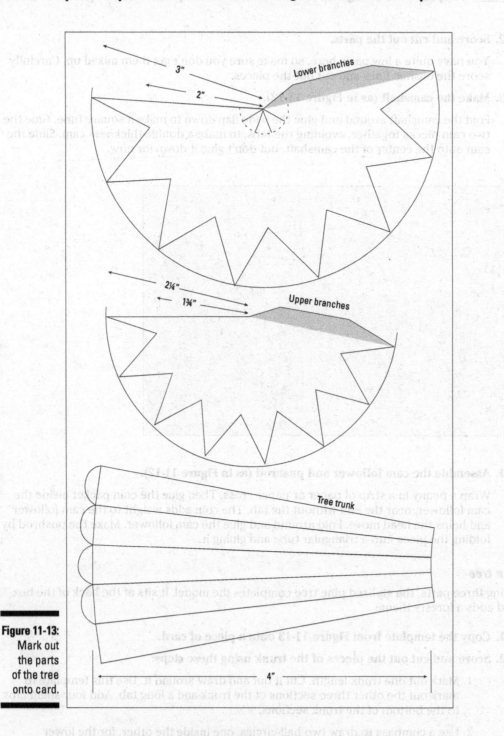

Figure 11-13:
Mark out
the parts
of the tree
onto card.

3. Fold the parts around and glue them.

Fold the trunk and glue it into shape. Each of the branch sections needs to be rolled into a cone shape like the ones in Figure 11-14. Cut a small tabbed hole in the center of the lower branches and thread them over the trunk. Glue them into place. Glue the upper branch cone to the top.

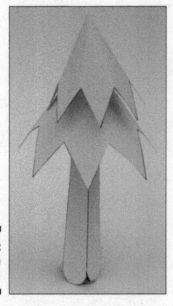

Figure 11-14:
Make the
tree!

Putting it all together

To complete the Nodding Moose model, you need to glue your parts together. This can be the fiddly part on some models, so take your time.

1. **Glue the pushrod to the bell crank inside the head.**

   Glue the pushrod so that the triangular section of the pushrod is facing forward toward the moose's nose.

2. **Glue the head to the neck.**

   The head glues to the neck part of the body, as shown in Figure 11-15. Make sure that the neck moves freely.

3. **Glue the moose to the box.**

   The front feet of the moose line up with the edge of the hole in the top of the box. Thread the pushrod down through the hole. Apply a thin layer of glue to the ends of the legs and glue them down to the top of the box

4. **Glue the cam follower into place.**

   The cam follower threads in from the back of the box. Glue one end to the back of the box and glue the pushrod to the other end as shown in Figure 11-16.

5. **Thread the camshaft into place in the box.**

   After the camshaft is in place, fix it with the two washers. Don't glue the washers for the moment so that you can experiment with different cams later on (see the next section, "Varying the moose's motion"). Slide the handle on the camshaft without gluing it.

6. **Finish the model off by adding the tree.**

   Two of the flaps on the tree trunk sit on top of the box, and the other two go on the sides of the box.

Figure 11-15:
Put all
the parts
together.

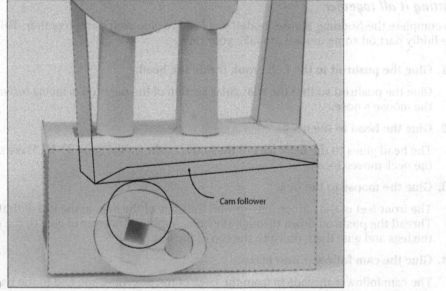

Cam follower

Figure 11-16:
The cam
follower
and cam.

Turn the handle, and the Nodding Moose agrees with everything you say. You can also try other kinds of animations with this simple mechanism, such as making a seagull that flaps its wings or a boat bobbing on the sea.

If you want to add color to the model, create the moose with suitable precolored cards (such as brown card for the moose's body) or color the model with colored pens (see Chapter 4 for details on adding color). I have a set of colored templates on my Web site at www. flying-pig.co.uk/dummies.

Varying the moose's motion

You can modify the moose model slightly by using a different cam profile. Try making a cam that's a long, thin oval shape like the first one in Figure 11-17. This shape has two lobes so it makes the moose nod twice as fast. You can add more and more lobes to your cam, but that can cause the cam follower to stop working properly. For a more complex cam, you need to add a finer end to your cam follower. Fortunately, this is easy to do: Just stick a triangular tube to the end, and your cam follower will work again. When you're happy with the cam, glue it to the camshaft and glue the washers and handle in place.

Figure 11-17:
Cams
and cam
followers.

Getting a Handle on a Better Working Winder

The part of the paper animation that takes the most wear is the handle, the part that the user turns to make the model work. In Chapter 10 and in the earlier moose project, I use simple types of handles. These basic types work just fine, but if you want to create a handle that's easier to turn, then try this one out. Handles have evolved over the years I've been doing paper automata, and this more-complex handle has a nice, curved surface to grip.

To replace the handle, first cut the old handle off your model by cutting the tabs off the end of the camshaft. Then follow these directions to make the replacement:

1. **Mark out the template for the handle from Figure 11-18, score along the dotted lines, and cut out the single piece that makes the handle.**

Figure 11-18:
Mark out
the handle
template
onto card.

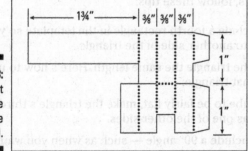

2. **Fold the two square tube sections around and glue them into place (see Figure 11-19a).**

   The dotted lines are valley folds, so fold the paper toward you.

3. **Fold the right-hand tube down so that it slots into the left-hand tube and glue it into place (see Figure 11-19b).**

4. **Roll the long tab around the handle and glue it down (see Figure 11-19c).**

5. **With the handle complete, glue it into place on the end of your camshaft.**

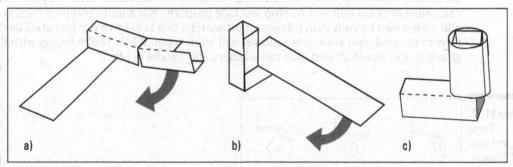

Figure 11-19:
Follow these steps to make a better handle.

a)   b)   c)

Using Triangles for Strength

Paper and card aren't what you'd consider strong materials. But although paper and card can tear easily, they're flexible. And with a little rolling, folding, and creasing, paper can be surprisingly strong. The secret is knowing the strengths of paper and exploiting those strengths.

Ask structural engineers, and they'll tell you that the triangle is a strong shape. Here's why: If you push on a shape that has more than three sides, such as a square, its corners can fold like hinges, changing the shape. But to distort a triangle, you'd have to actually bend or break its sides or joints. Triangles add strength because the only way you can change a triangle's shape is by changing the length of its sides.

That strength is why bridges, pylons, and scaffolding outside buildings all have many triangles in their structures. You can incorporate triangles in your paper engineering to strengthen your paper models. The most common triangular shape you use in paper engineering is the triangular tube, or *prism,* which has three sides made up of rectangles. To create a triangle and add strength to one of your projects, follow these tips:

✔ When making a triangular tube, include a fourth rectangle in the template so you can use it as a tab that you glue down to another side of the triangle.

✔ For simplicity, make two sides of the triangle the same length. Here's how to use the *third side* to change the shape of that triangle:

• If you want your triangular tube to be fairly flat, make the triangle's third side a little less than twice as long as one of the other sides.

• If you want your triangle to include a 90° angle — such as when you want to reinforce the edge of a box — make the third side 1.4 times as long as one of the other sides. (This works only if the other two sides are equal to each other, and it has to do with the Pythagorean Theorem. Take my word for it!)

Suppose you've designed a model with a large box top and you need to make sure that the top is rigid. You can add triangular sections on the back as Figure 11-20 shows.

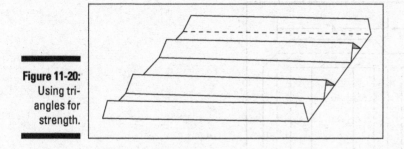

Figure 11-20:
Using triangles for strength.

You can also use the same technique to strengthen the inside of characters. Triangular tubes are surprisingly strong, and most of the pushrods in the models in this book use triangles. (The *pushrods* are the parts that connect one moving part to another; check out the earlier sections "In for a penny: Pushrod, cam, cam follower, and camshaft" and "Putting it all together" in the Nodding Moose project for an example.)

Designing a pushrod is straightforward; look at Figure 11-21. Notice that the center of the triangle is 1⅓ times as wide as two outer parts. This makes a nice, low-profile pushrod that's still strong.

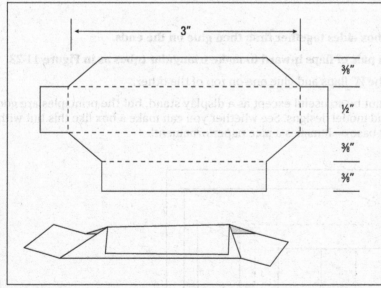

Figure 11-21:
Super strong pushrod.

Triangles can come in different forms. A narrow triangular tube is both rigid and strong. Instead of constructing a box from paper tubes, you can build the triangular tubes into the design of the paper box. This produces a strong, rigid box that's easy to make. Just follow these simple steps to make an example box:

1. **Copy the templates from Figure 11-22 onto thin card.**

    Notice that the ½" flap is about 1.4 times the width of the ⅜" border; this relationship creates a 90° angle when you put the box together.

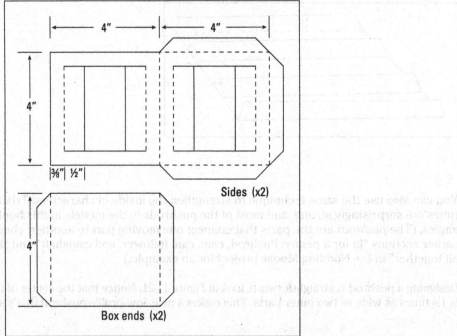

Figure 11-22:
Templates for a surprisingly strong box.

2. **Glue the box sides together first; then glue on the ends.**

3. **Fold each pair of flaps inward to make triangular tubes as in Figure 11-23.**

   Overlap the ½" flaps and glue one on top of the other.

This box may not be so useful except as a display stand, but the principles are good for other boxes and model designs. See whether you can make a box like this but with open sides, top, and base — it makes a nice paper ornament!

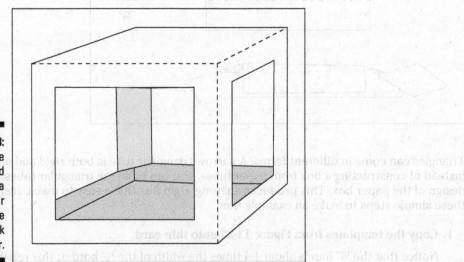

Figure 11-23:
The completed box, with a triangular tube visible at the back corner.

Chapter 12

Using Mechanisms to Bring Models to Life

In This Chapter

▶ Designing your models with movement in mind

▶ Making use of levers and linkages

▶ Creating a crank slider

▶ Using gears

Since ancient times, people have been fascinated by the idea of making machines that come to life. Inventors and automata makers have created all kinds of amazing machines, from models of people that can write their own names to archers that can draw a bow and fire an arrow. All these machines rely on *mechanisms,* the parts that make a machine work. In Chapters 10 and 11, I present projects that use the basic cam mechanism. In this chapter, I introduce you to crank sliders, gears, and levers, and I show you how you can use them in your paper engineering.

Giving Life to Your Models: The How-to

Paper animations, or paper *automata,* are models that move. In most paper animations, you turn a handle and the model appears to come to life; the more lifelike the movement, the better the model. In this section, I introduce some of the mechanisms you can use to create various types of movement and talk about using movement to add personality to your model.

 When you design a model, aim to make the movement of the model as different as possible from the movement of the user's hand. There should be a slight air of mystery and wonder as to how the character in the animation moves — this air of mystery is what makes paper automata so magical.

Understanding some common mechanisms

A *mechanism* is a collection of moving parts that are designed to do something, usually changing one kind of motion into another. For example, you can use a gear mechanism to slow down the motion from a rotating handle.

To design your own paper animations, you need to understand how some basic mechanisms work and what they do. Table 12-1 describes some of the mechanisms you may find in paper animations and what kinds of motion they can create. Later in this chapter, you can complete projects that feature the lever, crank slider, and gear mechanisms.

Table 12-1	Basic Mechanisms in Paper Animations	
Name	**Description**	**What It Does**
Cam	A wheel-like shape that rotates on a shaft and pushes against a cam follower	A cam lets you move another piece up and down. By changing the shape of the cam, you can change how your model moves (see Chapter 10).
Crank slider	A pushrod that fits through a slider tube (a sort of paper sleeve) and connects to a crankshaft	As the crankshaft turns, the pushrod moves up and down in a circular motion.
Gears	A set of interlocking toothed wheels	Gears can change the speed and direction of rotating motion.
Rack and pinion	A toothed wheel that meshes with a toothed bed	A rack and pinion converts rotating motion to straight-line motion.
Lever	A long piece that pivots on a single point	A lever can change the direction of travel, increase the strength of movement, or increase the speed of movement

Some lovely books on the subjects of mechanisms and how things work are available. You may want to add the following books to your library. They introduce you to all kinds of mechanisms that you can adapt for paper animations:

- ✔ *507 Mechanical Movements: Mechanisms and Devices,* by Henry T. Brown: This book is a reprint from a turn-of-the-century edition. It has lots of lovely drawings and diagrams of mechanisms in action.

- ✔ *Mechanisms and Mechanical Devices Sourcebook,* by Neil Sclater and Nicholas Chironis: This book is a real treat — but very expensive. Put it on your birthday list.

- ✔ *Cabaret Mechanical Movement: Understanding Movement and Making Automata,* by Aidan Lawrence Onn and Gary Alexander: This book is aimed at makers of traditional automata but has loads of ideas that you can adapt for paper animations.

Adding personality: Matching movement to your model

Almost all automata, whether they're made from paper or from more traditional materials such as wood and metal, have at least one character. Whether this is an animal or person doesn't matter; automata are there to tell a little story, and of course, stories need characters. To make the best automata, those characters need to have *character* — that is, personality! If you can give your paper creations attitude, that's what really brings them to life.

TIP

To give your paper animation model the personality that you're after, you need to choose the right movement. I always find it best to decide on the movement I'm after first and then try to figure out how I'm going to do it. If I start with the mechanism, I find myself thinking, "No, I can't do this, and I can't do that." But go the other way, and I'm often able to find a new and interesting way to make the movement I'm after. (See the preceding section for some of the mechanisms you can choose from.)

My model the Timid Tortoise (see Figure 12-1) is a case in point. My original idea was to make a model in which the tortoise poked her head out from her shell then drew it back in again. I was going to use a crank slider mechanism to wind the head in and out. A crank slider is a handy mechanism that I use quite a lot; basically, you turn the handle, and a piece at the top of the box pushes back and forth, like a piston. At that point, I was going to call the model something like What Kind of Day Is It Today? I'm sure I would've thought of something much more elegant and witty eventually, but you get the idea.

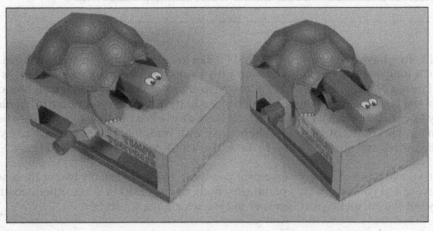

Figure 12-1:
The Timid
Tortoise.

A crank slider would've been fine, but it didn't really give the model any edge. I spent a bit more time thinking and sketching and eventually came up with the idea of the Timid Tortoise. In this model, the tortoise's head would come out slowly and nervously, get to a certain point, and then snap back inside her shell as if she'd been frightened. This gave the model an interesting character and allowed me to use a nicely alliterative name: The Timid Tortoise!

The final design drives the head out of the shell with a *rack and pinion* mechanism, a kind of toothed wheel that meshes with a toothed bed (see Figure 12-2); then a weight (some coins) snaps the head back. It's nice to watch people who know about mechanisms playing with this model. They have a go, and then they can't resist looking underneath the model to see how it all works. (***Note:*** To create your own rack and pinion mechanism, you can use some of the same paper-tooth-creating principles I introduce in the later section "Using Gears to Get You Going — or Slowing.")

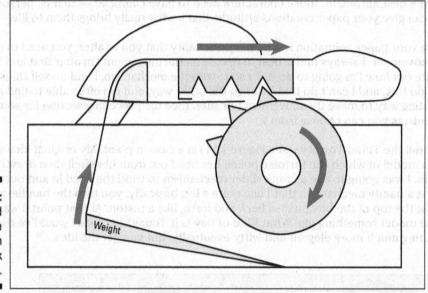

Figure 12-2:
The Timid
Tortoise
mechanism
uses a rack
and pinion.

Weight

I quite often have a few movements that I'd like to create to mull over in my head. If I think about it long enough, I usually come up with a solution. I've had a couple of ideas for a while that I haven't been able to crack. I'd love to design a model that has a small branch sticking out of the top of the box. On the branch sits a butterfly. When you turn the handle, the butterfly opens and closes its wings. So far, I haven't worked out how to build it — but I haven't given up. This butterfly model would be easy with traditional materials because you could use fine wires and strong springs to move the wings, but it's not so easy in card.

When you know what kind of movement you want, there are usually two or three ways of achieving it. If you have plenty of time, try both, or use LEGO or some other construction kit to try out the competing mechanisms and see which one works best.

Linking Clever Levers

The Greek mathematician and engineer Archimedes said that if you gave him a long enough lever and a place to stand, he could move the Earth. Levers are perhaps the simplest of all mechanisms, yet they're very useful. Not only do they link things together, but they also control the speed that they move and the power in the movement. In this section, I introduce the four-bar linkage, which is a set of connected levers, and I show you how to use it in a cool moneybox project.

Connecting levers with the four-bar linkage

Linkages are simply the means of joining parts of a mechanism together. In traditional automata, the linkages are made from rigid materials such as wood or metal. In paper engineering, the linkages still need to be rigid so that the linkage can push as well as pull. To make sure that the linkage is stiff, paper animations often use tubes, usually either triangular tubes or square tubes. By folding paper around into a tube and gluing it down, you make it surprisingly strong. However, for small parts, you may choose to use heavy card instead.

To make use of linkages, you need to be able to join parts together so that they can flex. In a paper model, you can make a simple hinge from a flap of paper.

The *four-bar linkage* is, as its name suggests, four bars joined together with some kind of hinge so that they're free to move as a set of interconnected levers. One of the bars is usually a fixed object. By changing the lengths of the linkages, you can make all kinds of interesting movements.

Project 12-1: Halloween Moneybox

This project uses a four-bar linkage (see the preceding section) to make a skull appear briefly when you put a coin in your Halloween moneybox. Figure 12-3 shows how the Halloween moneybox works. You drop the coin down the slot. As the coin bumps into the lower bar, the coin pushes the bar downward, raising the other end of the bar (lever) and lifting the skull into view on the back of the coffin-shaped box.

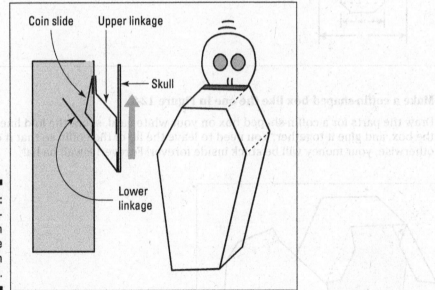

Figure 12-3:
A cross-section of the Halloween Moneybox.

Tools and Materials

3 sheets of white card

1 sheet of flexible paper

Pencil and eraser

Ruler

Scissors

Sharp craft knife

Cutting mat

White school glue and glue spreader

Two dimes

1. **Mark, score, and cut out the parts from the template (see Figure 12-4).**

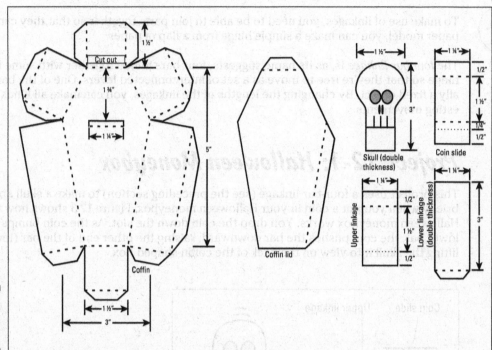

Figure 12-4:
The coffin
template.

2. **Make a coffin-shaped box like the one in Figure 12-5.**

   Draw the parts for a coffin-shaped box on your white card, score the fold lines, cut out the box, and glue it together. You need to leave the lid of the coffin so that it opens; otherwise, your money will be stuck inside forever! Forever! Mwah ha ha!

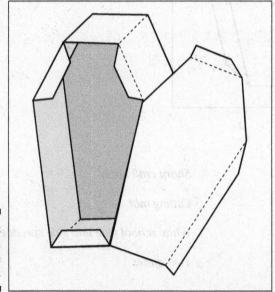

Figure 12-5:
Make a
coffin with
a lid.

3. **Make and attach the skull and four-bar linkage to the coffin box (Figure 12-3)**

   1. Glue the coin slide inside the coffin, just above the slit in the back.

   2. Glue the upper and lower linkages to the skull. Thread the lower linkage through the slit in the coffin. Glue the upper linkage to the outside of the coffin.

   3. Push on one end of the lower linkage to test its movement. When you're happy with it, use a flexible paper hinge to attach the lower linkage to the coffin.

4. **Wrap a couple of dimes in paper to use as weights and glue them to the bottom part of the skull.**

Trying the Crank Slider: A Rounded Flight Path

The *crank slider* is a useful mechanism. It works a bit like the piston in a car engine. As the crank turns, the pushrod moves up and down inside a slider tube, which is a kind of paper sleeve (see Figure 12-6). You can then attach the other end of the pushrod to your character or a part of your character.

The lower end of the pushrod moves in a circle. The shape made by the other end of the pushrod varies, depending on how long the pushrod is and where the slider tube is attached. This shape is known as a *locus*.

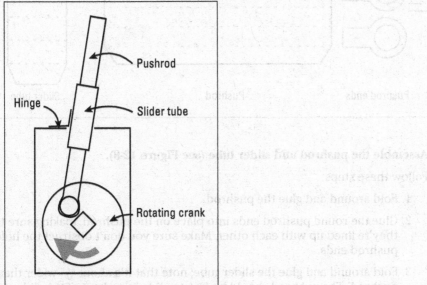

Figure 12-6:
The parts of the crank slider.

Pushrod

Hinge

Slider tube

Rotating crank

Building a crank slider

In this section, I show you how to craft a basic crank slider mechanism housed in a paper box. You can attach your character to the top of the pushrod. As you turn the handle in the box, the character moves in an oval-shaped locus — first up, then forward, then down, and finally back.

I show you how to make this mechanism in stages. You may need to experiment a little in fitting all the parts together. That's how we paper engineers do it!

Tools and Materials

Several sheets of thin white card

Ruler

Pencil and eraser

Scissors

Drawing compass

Sharp craft knife

Cutting mat

White school glue and glue spreader

1. **Mark and cut out the parts for the slider tube and pushrod (see Figure 12-7).**

   Mark the pushrod and slider tube parts onto your card and cut them out. Each pushrod end needs a circular hole cut into it, so use your compass. The hole needs to be big enough to fit a ³/₈" square tube through.

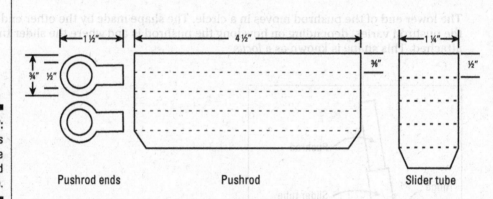

Figure 12-7: The parts for the pushrod and slider tube.

Pushrod ends   Pushrod   Slider tube

2. **Assemble the pushrod and slider tube (see Figure 12-8).**

   Follow these steps:

   1. Fold around and glue the pushrod.

   2. Glue the round pushrod ends into place on the pushrod, making sure that they're lined up with each other. Make sure you don't obstruct the holes in the pushrod ends.

   3. Fold around and glue the slider tube; note that it's about ¹/₈" wider than the main pushrod. The pushrod should be free to slide in and out of the slider tube — hence the name.

3. **Mark your card with the crankshaft templates and cut out the pieces.**

   You make the crankshaft from three square sections of ³/₈" cardboard tube. The middle section is a little shorter than the width of your box. See Figure 12-9. Cut out the pieces, fold them around, and glue them together.

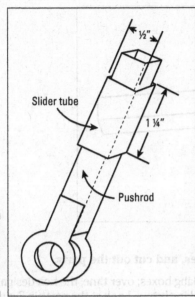

Figure 12-8:
Making the
pushrod and
slider tube.

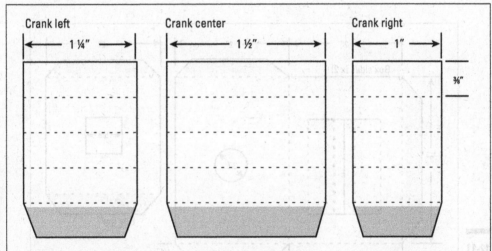

Figure 12-9:
The parts
for the
crankshaft.

4. **Put the pushrod on the crankshaft and glue the crankshaft together.**

   Here's how:

   1. Thread the crank center through the holes in the pushrod ends.

   2. Glue the other two parts of the crankshaft into place so that the pushrod is in the middle of the crank center and they're not quite touching the pushrod ends, as Figure 12-10 shows.

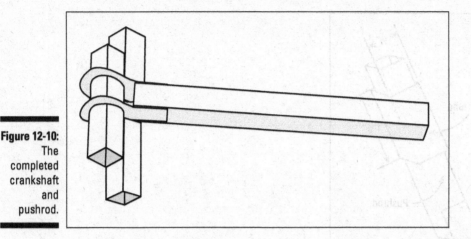

Figure 12-10:
The completed crankshaft and pushrod.

5. **Copy the box template, score the fold lines, and cut out the parts.**

   I like to experiment with different ways of making boxes; over time, the box design I've used has evolved, but here's my current way of making boxes. Look at the parts in Figure 12-11. You need two copies of the box sides and one top. This box doesn't have a separate base.

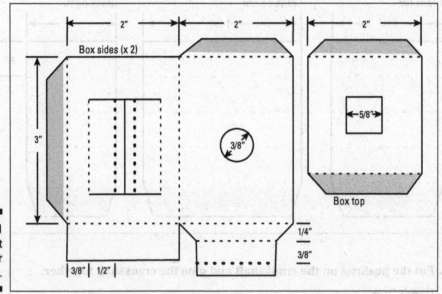

Figure 12-11
Mark out the parts for the box.

6. **Fold up the flaps as Figure 12-12 shows to make the base of the box.**

7. **Put the crankshaft in place and glue the box together.**

   Before you completely glue the box together, thread the crankshaft into place, putting the ends through the holes in the sides of the box. Fit the top to the box.

8. **Use a small flap of card to make a hinge that joins the slider tube to the top of the box (see Figure 12-13).**

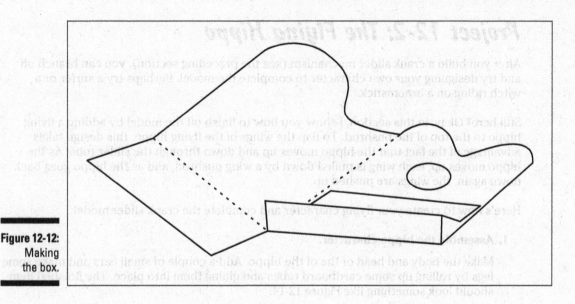

Figure 12-12:
Making
the box.

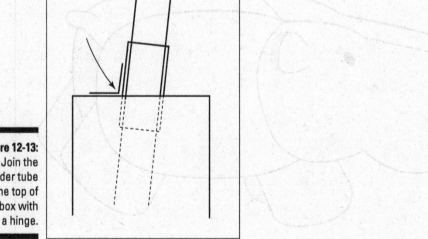

Figure 12-13:
Join the
slider tube
to the top of
the box with
a hinge.

9. Make a winder handle to go on the end of the crankshaft.

You may also like to add some washers to hold the crankshaft into place. These aren't usually necessary, but they can tidy up the look of the model. See Chapters 10 and 11 for projects using washers and handles, or make the more-advanced handle in Chapter 11.

You now have a completed crank slider, though at the moment it has no character. Try turning the handle to make sure that everything goes smoothly. If you see any problems, you may find that you have to carefully free things up with your sharp craft knife.

Project 12-2: The Flying Hippo

After you build a crank slider mechanism (see the preceding section), you can branch off and try designing your own character to complete the model. Perhaps try a surfer or a witch riding on a broomstick.

Still here? Okay, in this section, I show you how to finish off the model by adding a flying hippo to the top of the pushrod. To flap the wings of the flying hippo, this design takes advantage of the fact that the hippo moves up and down through the slider tube. As the hippo moves up, each wing is pulled down by a wing pushrod, and as the hippo goes back down again, the wings are pushed up.

Here's how to create your flying character and complete the crank slider model:

1. **Assemble the hippo character.**

   Make the body and head of the of the hippo. Add a couple of small ears and make some legs by rolling up some cardboard tubes and gluing them into place. The finished item should look something like Figure 12-14.

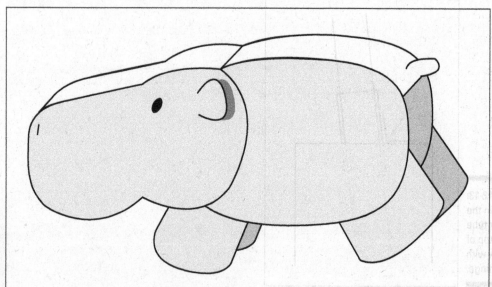

Figure 12-14:
The finished hippo. Not flying yet!

2. **Join the hippo to the top of the pushrod.**

   Add a couple of card flaps to the top of the pushrod. Then glue the pushrod up inside the body of the hippo. Turn the handle, and the hippo leaps through the air.

3. **Create two wings, a cross piece, and two wing pushrods.**

   The wing pushrods are the parts that make the wings move up and down. Look at Figure 12-15 for the bits you need to make.

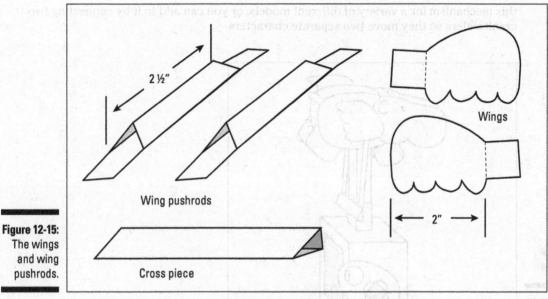

Figure 12-15:
The wings
and wing
pushrods.

Wings

2 ½"

Wing pushrods

2"

Cross piece

4. Glue the wings, cross piece, and wing pushrods into place.

The wings join to the body using a cardboard hinge.

Glue the cross piece to the slider tube, point up. One end of each wing pushrod attaches to the cross piece; the other end of the pushrod attaches to a wing. Look at Figure 12-16 to see how it all fits together.

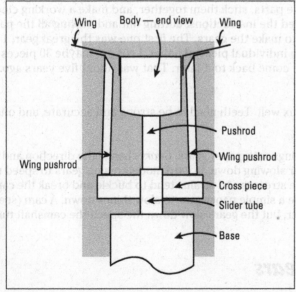

Figure 12-16:
Fitting
together
the wings
and wing
pushrods.

Wing — Body — end view — Wing

Pushrod

Wing pushrod

Wing pushrod

Cross piece

Slider tube

Base

When your model is all together, it should look something like the one in Figure 12-17. Making this model can give you a good insight into how a crank slider works. You can use this mechanism for a variety of different models, or you can add to it by connecting two crank sliders so they move two separate characters.

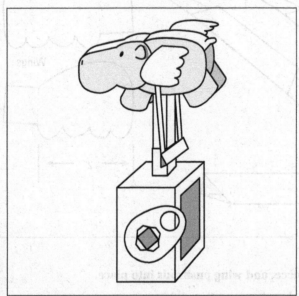

Figure 12-17: The finished hippo

Using Gears to Get You Going — or Slowing

A good friend of mine once gave me a make-your-own paper clock kit. The idea of the kit was that you cut out all the parts, stick them together, and make a working clock. Fascinating! I carefully followed the instructions, cutting out and making all the parts of the clock case. Then it was time to make the gears. The first one was the great gear, 144 teeth. Each tooth was made from an individual piece of paper. I cut out maybe 30 pieces and then put it to one side, thinking I'd come back to it later. That was about five years ago. Perhaps I'll finish it when I retire.

Gears and card really don't mix well. Teeth need to be strong and accurate, and often you need to have loads of them.

However, you can do a few things with paper gears. *Gears* change the direction and speed of rotation, either speeding up or slowing down. In card models, using gears to speed up rotation isn't really possible — the stresses and strains tend to buckle and break the card. In this section, I show you how to use a simple paper gear to slow things down. A cam (see Chapter 10) moves the actual character, but the gears slow down the speed the camshaft turns.

Making paper gears

You can make paper gears a few different ways. The way I show you here is fairly simple, and it doesn't take weeks and weeks to make. Look at Figure 12-18 to see the principle of the paper gear. Each gear turns on a shaft. The teeth on the smaller gear are made of triangular tubes of paper attached directly to the shaft. The larger gear is double-thickness card with the teeth cut out of it.

In this model, the smaller gear has only 4 teeth; the large gear has 12. When you turn the small gear, the large gear turns at $^4/_{12}$, or $^1/_3$, of the speed.

In addition to some card, a pencil, scissors, a ruler, white school glue, and the other standard paper-engineering supplies, you need a drawing compass and protractor so you can correctly draw and measure the the teeth. The following sections explain how to make the gear mechanism.

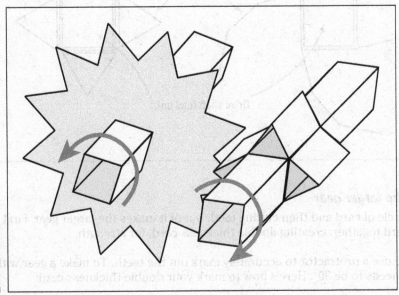

Figure 12-18:
Simple
paper gears.

Creating the small gear

To create the small gear, first make a drive shaft from a $^3/_8$" square tube approximately 3" long. Each tooth is made from a strip of card, $^3/_4$" x $^3/_8$", as the template in Figure 12-19 shows.

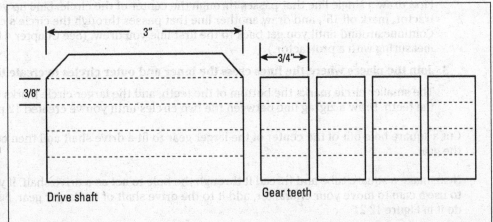

Figure 12-19:
The parts
for the
small gear.

Attach the four tooth pieces to the drive shaft as Figure 12-20 shows.

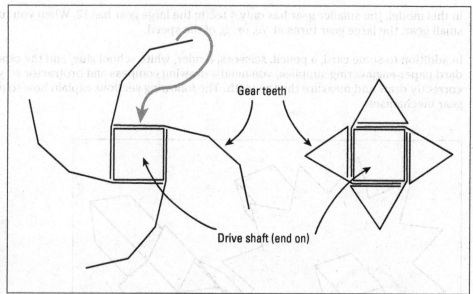

Gear teeth

Drive shaft (end on)

Figure 12-20:
Making the
small gear.

Creating the larger gear

Making a circle of card and then cutting teeth out of it makes the larger gear. First glue two pieces of card together, creating double-thickness card, for strength.

You need to use a protractor to accurately mark out the teeth. To make a gear with 12 teeth, each tooth needs to be 30°. Here's how to mark your double-thickness card:

1. **Use a drawing compass to draw two circles, an inner circle and an outer circle.**

   For the smaller circle, make the radius (the distance between the compass points) 2". The larger circle has a radius of 2½".

2. **At every 15°, draw a line that goes through the center of the large circle, like the spokes of a wheel.**

   First draw a single line that passes through the center of the circle. Line up your protractor, mark off 15°, and draw another line that passes through the circle's center. Continue around until you get back to the first line you drew. (See Chapter 4 for tips on measuring with a protractor.)

3. **Join the places where the lines cross the inner and outer circles to create the teeth.**

   The smaller circle marks the bottom of the teeth, and the larger circle marks the top of the teeth. Draw a zigzag line between the two circles until you've created 12 points.

Cut a square hole out of the center of the larger gear to fit a drive shaft and then cut out the gear.

Next, make a square tube and thread it through the hole to act as a drive shaft. If you want to use a cam to move your character, add it to the drive shaft of the larger gear. See how to do it in Figure 12-21.

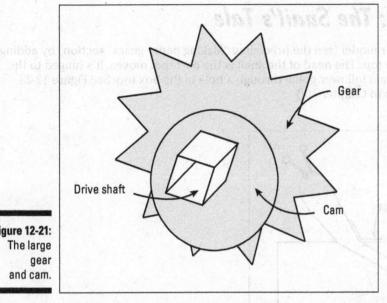

Figure 12-21:
The large gear and cam.

Constructing a box that fits the size of the gears

After making your small and large gears (see the preceding sections), hold the two gears together to see how far apart the shafts need to be. You can then use this information to construct a box. Make the box as Figure 12-22 shows and assemble it around the gears.

I usually like to have holes in the box so you can see how the mechanism works. You can add these to the end of the box if you like. See Chapters 10 and 11 for more on boxes.

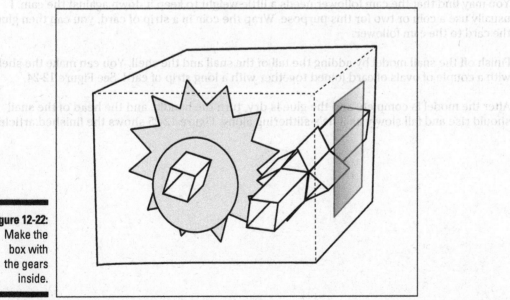

Figure 12-22:
Make the box with the gears inside.

Project 12-3: The Snail's Tale

You can finish off a gear model (see the preceding "Making paper gears" section) by adding a snail character to the top. The head of the snail is the part that moves. It's hinged to the top of the box, with a cam follower going through a hole in the box top. See Figure 12-23. (For more on cams, flip to Chapter 10.)

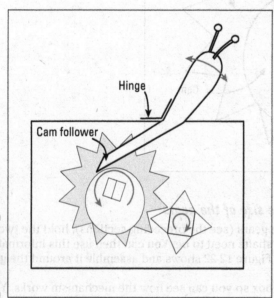

Figure 12-23: The moving head of the snail.

You may find that the cam follower needs a little weight to keep it down against the cam. I usually use a coin or two for this purpose. Wrap the coin in a strip of card; you can then glue the card to the cam follower.

Finish off the snail model by adding the tail of the snail and the shell. You can make the shell with a couple of ovals of card joined together with a long strip of card. See Figure 12-24.

After the model is complete and the glue is dry, turn the handle, and the head of the snail should rise and fall slowly as if he's slithering along. Figure 12-25 shows the finished article.

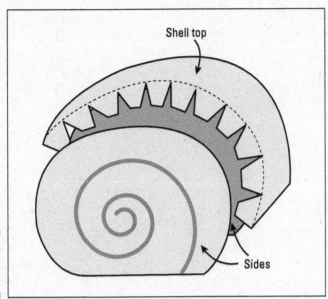

Shell top

Sides

Figure 12-24:
Making the
snail shell.

Figure 12-25:
The finished
Snail's Tale
paper
animation.

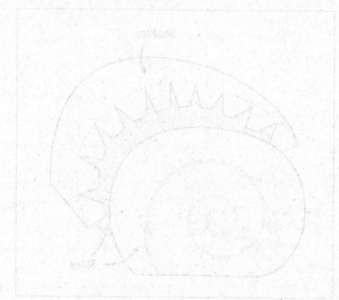

Figure 12-24: Making the snail shell

Figure 12-25: The finished Snail's Tale paper animation

Part IV
Drafting Your Own Designs and Creations

The 5th Wave   By Rich Tennant

"Exactly what kind of pop-up project <u>are</u> you designing?"

In this part . . .

After you grasp the basics of paper engineering, you may want to create your own designs. In this part, I guide you through the process, from generating good ideas to recording those ideas and keeping a notebook. I talk about how to choose the right color scheme and how to build from sketches. To take your designs to the next level, you can use computers to help you with your new hobby. I tell you about free software you can use and where to get it. I also give you a quick starter guide on how to use it. And if you have a real knack for designing and making projects, you may want to consider selling your product. If so, this part also has a chapter to help you with that decision.

Chapter 13

Developing Your Own Designs

- -

In This Chapter

▶ Putting ideas in a notebook

▶ Sketching your plans

▶ Building from your blueprints

- -

The transformation from a set of instructions on a page to a finished project can be quite satisfying. However, you may have reached the point where you want to create your own designs. Perhaps you can't find a template for what you want to make, or maybe you're just feeling creative.

Making your own design is more difficult than following instructions in a book, but if you're ready for the challenge, this chapter guides you through the design process.

Coming Up with and Recording Design Ideas

Where do ideas come from? This question has always been a bit of a mystery. In ancient times, people thought that ideas came to them when they were visited by a Muse — a kind of ideas spirit. Even now it can seem a bit of a magical process — you can wake up in the night with a really good idea (though it's usually less impressive in the cold light of day!), or ideas may come to you throughout the day.

Each person is unique, so I don't have any magical potion to make ideas pop into your head. However, this section does point out a few suggestions you can use to encourage your creativity. It also explains why recording all your ideas in one central location is important.

Putting your ideas in a notebook

You've probably experienced coming up with a great idea when you didn't have a pen and paper; by the time you got home, you'd forgotten what it was. To remember your best paper-engineering design ideas, I suggest you describe or draw your ideas in a notebook.

I used to write down ideas and plans on scraps of paper, backs of train tickets, or receipts from shops. The problem is that all those bits of paper are easy to lose, and if you have a memory as skatty as mine, as soon as the note is gone, the idea is gone.

Keep a notebook close at hand so that whenever an idea pops into your mind, you can quickly write it down. I carry a notebook with me at all times. That's not to say that I have ideas all the time — I often go for days without writing or drawing anything — but if you don't have your notebook, you can't write anything down.

To find a good notebook, check out the selection at your local arts and crafts shop or local stationery store. In many ways, choosing a notebook is a matter of personal preference. Notebooks come in many shapes and sizes, but here are the main choices you have and a bit about each one to help you decide:

✔ **Perfect bound versus spiral bound:** *Perfect binding* is the binding used in traditional types of books like this one. Pages are grouped in *signatures,* folds of about six sheets of paper; several signatures are then grouped together and bound into a book. Spiral bound notebooks use a spiral wire or plastic combs to group pages together.

Perfect bound notebooks have the advantage that you can draw or write right across a double-page spread. The notebooks are also more robust than spiral bound books. Spiral bound notebooks have the advantage that they can be opened fully and will sit with their pages open on your desk.

✔ **Large or small:** Most notebooks are letter-size (8½" x 11") or smaller — some are small enough to fit in a pocket or purse. A large notebook lets you fit lots on a page and allows you to draw big. A small notebook is portable and unobtrusive. I tend to have a large, letter-size notebook that I keep at home and a smaller pocket-size book that I carry around with me.

✔ **Lined or unlined:** Notebook pages come in a variety of finishes, from the simple plain paper to paper printed with lines or a dot grid. Unless you're doing lots of writing, I recommend using plain paper because it's a clear space to record your ideas.

I tend to go for a large, letter-size notebook that gives me plenty of room for drawing. I like to use perfect bound books so that I can draw across the double-page spread, as you can see in Figure 13-1. I also use plain paper rather than lined.

Figure 13-1:
A double-page spread in a perfect bound notebook.

In addition to using your notebook as a way to record and sketch your design ideas, you can use it as a scrapbook and collect scraps and samples you encounter. I collect all kinds of clippings and pictures that I find interesting. Most of them aren't directly related to paper engineering, but I collect color schemes that I like and pictures I find interesting or attractive. Very occasionally, I clip written articles that I like and put them in my notebook. Look for materials online or in magazines. After you glue a picture or article in your notebook, write a short note next to it reminding you why you were interested in this piece and what thoughts and ideas it triggered.

You can use your computer to act as an electronic scrapbook. Use Jing (www.jingproject. com) to take snapshots of interesting things on your screen and save them online. It's free and easy to use.

Warming up your thinking machine

Creativity is mostly a matter of connecting ideas in new ways. Those ideas may be related, or you may bring together two images you never thought you'd picture together (lobsters and tennis, anyone?). In this section, I name a few ways you can boost your creativity and come up with design ideas for your projects.

Researching other people's ideas — and revisiting your own

In the world of art, there's a long tradition of looking back at what other people have created and expanding on it. Don't be afraid of looking at the work of other paper engineers in search of inspiration. You're not cheating or copying unless you directly copy their work. Feel free to adapt an element or mechanism you see into your own design.

For instance, you may want to take a sneak peek at this crew of "cardboard engineers" for inspiration on just how far you can take the skills you pick up in this book (www.cardboardinstitute.com). Make sure you revisit some of the ideas you've collected in your notebook as well (see the preceding section for tips on keeping a notebook).

Keeping your eyes open

Don't limit yourself — you can find sources of inspiration all around you; you just need to keep your eyes open to see them! Don't just look at the obvious things, though; watch out for the surprises.

For example, if you're thinking up ideas for a paper-engineered wedding invitation, then as you're walking around the mall, keep an eye open for ideas you can use. Keep looking while you're watching TV, and don't stop looking while you're walking in the park. You'll be surprised at what triggers an idea. A jigsaw may give you the idea of making wedding invitations as two puzzle pieces that make a whole. Seeing a cup in a coffee shop may make you think cup→drink, drink→glass, and glass→champagne, so you decide to make a 3D champagne flute.

Mixing different ideas to make something new

Juxtaposition involves linking two normally unconnected ideas to create a third, often quite creative new idea. For example, I've always been interested in electronics and the inner workings of computers. I had an idea that it'd be fun to try to make a logic gate (the basis of the microprocessor) from paper and had worked out a few mechanisms. But it wasn't until I combined the idea of logic *gates* with *goats* that my Logic Goats range of paper models was born.

Here are a few ways you can juxtapose ideas and come up with some new combinations:

- ✔ **Use your memories and stories.** Because of your experiences, you may already have some strange associations in your head.

- ✔ **Take advantage of accidental combinations.** Sometimes you find ideas; and sometimes, ideas find you. Dreams are notorious for putting together images that don't completely make sense. Or you may come up with ideas when you mishear someone. Don't intentionally half-listen to people (you'll get in trouble), but be ready to reap the rewards of your mistakes — or immortalize your friends' mistakes in a pop-up card!

- ✔ **Picture what people are saying.** The English language has lots of phrases that can give you interesting mental pictures if you take them literally. In that way of thinking, the "Man in the Moon" is a spaceman who lives in a crater, "turning the tables on someone" involves spinning furniture, and a "dry run" means jogging through the desert. For example, I took the idea of "surfing the Web" and linked it with the idea of a spider on his web to come up with the paper animation model Surfin' the Web (Figure 13-2).

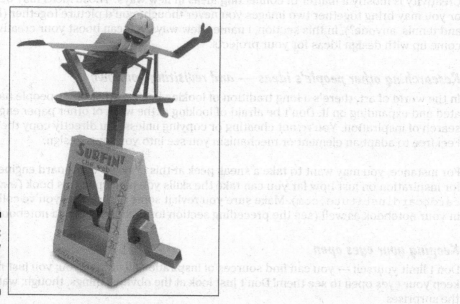

Figure 13-2:
Literally
surfing the
Web.

Doodling on paper — and with paper

A good way to come up with ideas is to throw images together and see what happens. Whenever you have a free moment, open a notebook and sketch. If you're in a boring meeting, on the train, or watching TV, spend some time sketching. Doodling doesn't need to have a theme or subject; it's just about making marks on paper that you can use.

You can create 3D doodles by spending your free time cutting out shapes and gluing them together to see how they work. As you do this, you can discover loads about what shapes work and which don't. Don't forget to keep your best 3D doodles so you can use the ideas later.

Brainstorming design ideas

Your brain and memory work by making connections between different thoughts and ideas. With brainstorming, you take these connections and map them on paper. The idea is to get everything down on paper before you make your judgments; don't censor as you write — just get it all down there. Brainstorming is useful when you already have a subject or theme in mind but you don't know exactly what you want to make.

Take time to brainstorm. To come up with ideas, follow these steps:

1. **Write down the subject of your project and begin to list all the things that come to mind when you think of that subject.**

   Whatever the subject may be, such as a birthday, holidays, congratulations, or whatever, make a list. For example, when you think of birthdays, you may list *balloons, cake, ice cream, presents, party, streamers,* and so on. At this stage, don't worry about getting things right or wrong. (Check out the earlier section "Putting your ideas in a notebook" for more about keeping ideas in one place.)

2. **After you write down a few ideas, narrow them down and pick out what you think may be the best ideas.**

   Pick a couple of good ideas from your list. To help you choose between them, make some sketches of both ideas, and think about how you could make these into a pop-up or other paper-engineering project.

After you have an idea of the project that you want to make, spend a bit of time making a good quality sketch of the finished design. See the later section "Understanding the Fine Art of Sketching" for more on drawing your design.

Choosing colors

Color can be the extra dimension that finishes off your design. Choosing the right color can make the difference between an average design and a really classy model. So as you're coming up with ideas, make sure you keep in mind your different color options.

When collecting photos and pictures for ideas, also collect interesting color schemes. That way, when you're finishing your design, you'll have a collection of colors to choose from.

The Internet is a great place to help you come up with color schemes. Check out the following Web sites to help you with your color options. You may be surprised at all the shades and hues available:

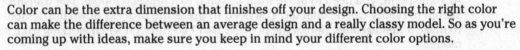

✔ **Kuler (kuler.adobe.com):** Kuler (pronounced *color*) is a fabulous resource showing all kinds of ways of mixing and matching colors. One of my favorites!

✔ **Colr (www.colr.org):** Colr is an interesting tool. Show the Web site a photo, and it creates a color scheme from it. Cool!

✔ **ColorExplorer (www.colorexplorer.com):** Hey, this one has real words spelled right! ColorExplorer has all kinds of interesting tools for mixing and matching colors.

Understanding the Fine Art of Sketching

Drawing your ideas in a notebook lets you start to visualize your project. After you decide on the idea for the project you want to make, do a little planning and make some detailed sketches.

To start, I suggest you make sketches of different aspects of your design. If your project is mechanical, then spend a little time sketching to work out the details of the mechanism. If you have a character in your project, then sketch what he or she looks like. Try a few different designs and choose the one that you're happiest with. Finally, as you get closer to completing your design, spend some time sketching out parts and adding dimensions and measurements to your diagrams.

If you're not confident in your drawing abilities, don't worry. To help you start to sketch and doodle, keep the following pointers in mind:

✔ **Copy.** Your teacher may have scolded your for copying your friend's homework, but when sketching, there's nothing wrong with copying. Remember that you're simply trying to put ideas on paper.

✔ **Practice.** Drawing is like any other skill. The more you practice, the better you get. Try to visualize what you're drawing before you put pencil to paper. Look at the paper, imagine what you want to draw, and then draw around your imagination. If you make a mistake, just erase it. Keep on practicing, and you'll be surprised at what you can achieve.

✔ **Relax and go with the flow.** Your sketches don't have to be perfect. You're not sketching for anyone but yourself to help you put your idea into something you can see, so don't worry.

Making the Transition from Sketch to Model

At some point, you need to move from a sketch to a finished model. The transition from sketch to reality can be difficult. You need to break the process down into simple steps to make it manageable. Here's the process that I go through when working from sketch to model:

1. **Create sketches from a number of different points of view.**

   The more you understand what you're aiming to create, the easier the transition from sketch to model will be. Try to make your sketches life size. (*Note:* That's the size of the final model, not the size of a real bear or whatever character you're making.)

2. **Draw any of the flat shapes within the design onto card and cut them out.**

3. **Glue the flat shapes together to try to make a 3D version of your sketch.**

   Don't worry if the model looks scruffy at this stage.

4. **Keep adding bits to the model and cutting bits off as appropriate.**

   Gradually, you achieve a sort of Frankenstein's monster version of the finished model.

5. **When you're happy with the finished shape, cut the whole thing apart, lay it flat on your workbench, and make copies.**

   Trace all the parts or, if you have a scanner, scan them into your computer.

6. **Lay the pieces you designed out on a piece of card as a set of templates.**

   Trace the templates, and you're ready to make them into a model.

Chapter 14

Using Technology to Design Your Own Projects

. . . .

In This Chapter

▶ Understanding how computers can help you in paper engineering

▶ Identifying and using helpful software

. . . .

Computer programs have come a long way in the world of design. About 15 years ago, technology appropriate for designing paper-engineering projects would've been unavailable, impractical, or way too expensive for the everyday designer. Today, you're in luck. If you know your way around a mouse pad, several programs can help you with your design and finishing touches. Even better, some of these programs are free and easy to use. There's no need to join the other engineers and sign up for a course in computer-aided design (CAD) — you get to play with some great photo-editing and drawing programs.

If you're tech savvy and want to use a computer to help take your paper-engineering designs to the next level, this chapter is a good starting point. Here I discuss how computers can assist you, and I name some of the more common programs.

Understanding How Your Computer Can Help with Your Design

Computers can help you with your paper-engineering design, but they can't do the actual design work. For getting your ideas down, you can't beat the simple paper and pencil. After you get the general idea on paper (see Chapter 13 for tips), you can finish off on the computer. The immediacy and ease of just drawing is perhaps the most natural way of starting your design process.

So what can a computer do for you? Computers are great for when you're trying out a design idea or finishing up a project. Here are a few practical ways to use a computer:

✔ **Tweaking a design:** You can easily make small changes without having to redraw everything. Using your computer, you can change a color scheme or resize a part quickly and easily, courtesy of the onscreen rulers and grids.

Printing large areas of color can use a lot of expensive ink. I complete my designs in white with black outlines before moving to the color stage.

✔ **Decorating paper:** You can create patterns and edit photos to print on the card you'll use to make your final project.

✔ **Archiving templates:** Keep a copy of templates so you can replicate a design. You can draw templates directly in a computer program or scan in parts of your disassembled project.

When I'm designing a new animation kit, I usually sketch out parts onto card, cut them out, and stick them together; when I'm happy with the shape, I open it out, put the parts in my scanner, and transfer it to the computer.

Making templates in a computer program can be especially useful as you refine your design. For example, I had an idea to design a paper animation kit featuring a sheep in a boat — called a Ewe Boat, of course! See Figure 14-1 for the finished project.

I wanted to turn a handle and have the sheep in the boat row her oars. I made a prototype. It worked, but I wanted the model to look like she was really *pulling* on the oars. I made a few changes, and it was a little better but still not quite right. In the end, I'd created a whole fleet of ewe boats before I got the movement just right. Creating all these variations was possible because I'd designed the model on my computer. I was able to change the length of a pushrod here, alter the throw of a crank there, and then just print the parts out and try the model again. Imagine if I had to measure out and draw each and every prototype with a pencil and ruler. I'd still be working on that model now.

Figure 14-1:
The final version of the Ewe Boat.

Relying on Software to Help with Your Rendering

Several types of software are available to assist you with your paper-engineering designs. No matter what your abilities are or how much money you want to spend (if any), you can use software to fine-tune your renderings. With some fairly basic computer equipment, you can create professional looking paper models. And although you can spend a fortune on professional software, you don't actually have to. You can go online and download free, open source software that can produce superb results.

Open source software is software developed by teams of programmers who give their time for free to produce high-quality tools that are available to everybody (and if you're really into computers, you're free to modify the software and even distribute it, as long as you give other people access to the code you started with). Open source programs usually have a strong community of helpful users, so if you get stuck, you can almost always get an answer to your question by visiting an online help forum, sometimes within minutes of asking the question. This software is available for all kinds of purposes. Luckily, a good range of software is suitable for the paper engineer.

If you have money to spend on software, look no further than the Adobe Creative Suite of programs. You need a deep wallet, but these programs are the tools of the pros. Their features are similar to those of the open source programs that you can use for free, but they have much more polish. The interface is better, and in some areas, such as handling text, the professional programs are much more powerful. You can download a free 30-day trial of these programs from the Adobe Web site (www.adobe.com/products) to give them a sample go.

Not sure what kinds of software you may need? No worries. This section covers both some free and not-so-free software that you may want to try to make your paper-engineering designs stick out above the rest. I also provide some steps to help you experiment with the open source versions. If you're just beginning your paper engineering and don't have the budget to buy expensive software, stick with the freebies in this chapter first. If you sample the professional products and want to purchase them, go for it — just follow the software's instructions for the basics.

Drawing the line: Software for templates and color experiments

When designing templates for your paper models, you need a program that lets you draw shapes on a screen. You want to be able to tweak the shapes by changing the width or perhaps moving a corner. To finish off your design, you also want to be able to add some color and then easily change the color if you decide you don't like it. The perfect program for this kind of work is the vector-based art package. *Vector* is simply a computer word for *line*, so a vector package is a program to let you draw and edit lines.

Opting for open source with Inkscape

If you plan to create templates and experiment with color on your model, Inkscape fits the bill perfectly. And because it's open source, it's absolutely free. Go to www.inkscape.org to download Inkscape. After you have it installed, it opens a window like the one in Figure 14-2 (minus the stars and spiral — you have to draw those yourself).

The following information is a quick step-by-step introduction to Inkscape. Inkscape is a very powerful program that can do all sorts of amazing things, such as create superb posters or design beautiful business cards, as well as make professional quality paper-engineering projects. With a bit of practice, you'll soon become fluent in its use. Just keep trying and don't worry — you can always undo your mistakes.

If you run into trouble, just click on Help⇨Tutorials for a whole range of lessons on using Inkscape. If you're still stuck, ask the helpful people at www.inkscapeforum.com or another Inkscape forum.

Figure 14-2:
The
Inkscape
window.

Figure 14-3 shows a template of the type of part you may want to create in Inkscape. This is a pushrod like the ones in Chapter 12. Follow these instructions to see how to make it:

1. Open a new document in Inkscape.

To do so, click on File⇨New⇨Letter to create a letter-size page. You can choose from loads of page size options, but for this example, I stick with letter.

2. Turn on the grid.

Go to View⇨Grid and then to View⇨Snap. This puts a grid pattern on your screen and attaches the lines you draw to the grid. The grid makes it easy to draw accurate lines.

3. Zoom in to page width.

Use the + key on your keyboard to zoom in so you can see one page width. If you zoom in too far, use the – key to zoom back out.

4. Select the Draw Bezier Curves and Straight Lines tool (refer to the upper right corner of Figure 14-4) and draw the basic outline of your shape.

Move your mouse pointer to where you want a corner to be and click. Work your way around the shape. When you get back to the beginning, a closed shape, as in Figure 14-7, appears. You can change the color of the shape by clicking on the color boxes at the bottom of the screen.

5. Try moving the shape around the page.

Click on the Select tool. This tool looks like an arrow, just like your mouse pointer. Click on the shape and then try dragging and dropping it around the screen.

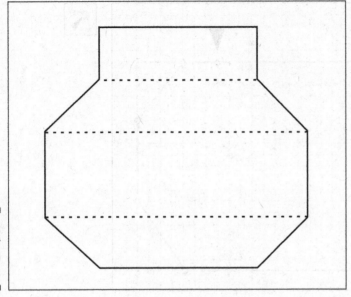

Figure 14-3:
A paper
pushrod
template.

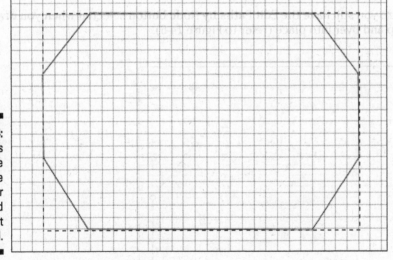

Figure 14-4:
Draw this
basic shape
with the
Draw Bezier
Curves and
Straight
Lines tool.

6. Add some more nodes to the shape.

Nodes are simply points on the line. Think of them as corners.

You can grab hold of a node and move it to change the shape on your screen. Select the Edit Paths by Nodes tool and click on the edge of the shape to select it. Double click where you want the new nodes to appear as in Figure 14-5.

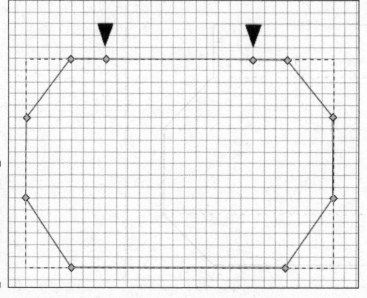

Figure 14-5:
Add two
new nodes
here with
the Edit Path
by Nodes
tool.

7. Click and drag the new nodes into position.

Make sure you still have the Edit Paths by Node button selected when you drag the nodes up and over into place (refer to Figure 14-6).

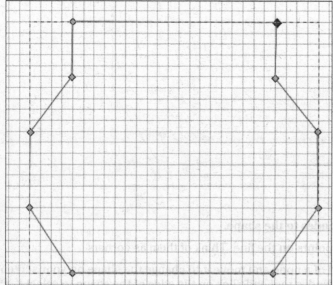

Figure 14-6:
Drag the
nodes into
place.

8. Add the fold lines (see Figure 14-7).

When working on templates, I use solid lines as cut lines and dashed lines to show where to crease. To make fold lines, start with three solid horizontal lines by selecting the Draw Bezier Curves and Straight Lines Tool, clicking the beginning point of the line, moving the pointer, and double-clicking the end of the line.

9. Make the fold lines dashed.

In a vector-based program like Inkscape, the color of an object is called the *fill* and the line around an object is called the *stroke*.

Using the Select tool, select a horizontal line by clicking on it. Right click on the line and select Fill and Stroke. A dialogue box pops up (as in Figure 14-7). Click on the Stroke Style tab and choose the dash style that you want from the Dashes drop-down list. Click on OK. Do this for each of the three horizontal lines.

While you have the Fill and Stroke window open, try out some of the other available effects. If you do anything wrong, you can just press Ctrl+Z to undo your mistake. (If only life had Ctrl+Z buttons!)

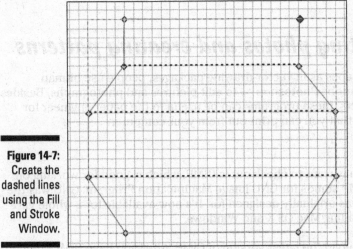

Figure 14-7: Create the dashed lines using the Fill and Stroke Window.

Going pro with Adobe Illustrator

I do most of my design work with Adobe Illustrator (www.adobe.com/products/ illustrator). Illustrator is a vector-drawing package — basically a piece of software that lets you draw lines and shapes and then edit them. It also has powerful tools for arranging text on a page. This means that graphic designers often use it to produce book covers or brochures. Figure 14-8 shows a typical Illustrator document.

For more in-depth, how-to information, check out the latest version of *Illustrator For Dummies* by Ted Alspach (Wiley).

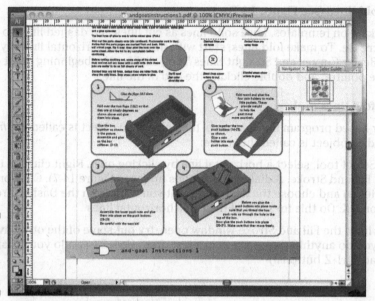

Figure 14-8:
Adobe
Illustrator in
action.

Software for editing photos and creating patterns

Instead of editing lines and shapes as in vector-drawing packages, people use bitmap editors — such as GIMP and Adobe Photoshop — to edit pictures and photographs. Besides editing photos for your projects, these programs can be useful to the paper engineer for making textures and patterns that you can print out from your computer.

Getting GIMP for free

A open source program you may want to check out is GIMP, which is good for working on photographs and designs. GIMP stands for GNU Image Manipulation Program. GNU was the operating system that GIMP was originally designed for. It's now available for a whole variety of operating systems, including Mac OS X and Windows.

Go to www.gimp.org to download the latest version of GIMP. After you have GIMP running, follow these steps to try out some of its pattern-making functions:

1. **Create a new document.**

   Click on File➪New. Set the image size to 450 x 300 and click on OK. You should see something like Figure 14-9.

2. **Fill your page with a pattern.**

   You can use GIMP to fill an object on the screen with color or with a pattern. Go to Dialogues➪Patterns to open the pattern dialogue box (see Figure 14-10). You can see the pattern names by clicking on them. After you find the pattern you want, click on Edit➪Fill with Pattern. For this exercise, try Parque #2.

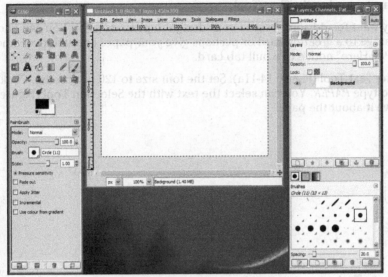

Figure 14-9:
The GIMP
work area.

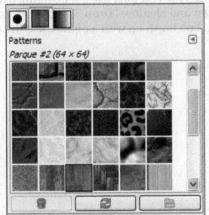

Figure 14-10:
Select the
Parque #2
pattern.

3. Apply a filter to play around with pattern effects.

One common filter allows you to blur the photo or pattern, making it look out of focus. To blur, click on Filters⇨Blur⇨Motion Blur. I chose a length of 120 and an angle of 30, but you can experiment for different effects. You now have a nice, soft wood effect as a background for your text.

The Blur tool is just one of the many special-effects filters that come with GIMP. You can also add an embossed effect to your art, add a drop shadow, or pixelate your image. You can find loads more at the GIMP reference guide at docs.gimp.org/en/filters.

4. Add some text using the Text Tool.

You may want to add some text to your design to personalize it. You can add a birthday message to a greeting card or perhaps give your paper animation a name or simply add a "Pull Here" notice to a pull-tab card.

Select the Text Tool (Figure 14-11a). Set the font size to 120 px (pixels). Click on the page and type *PAPER*. You can select the text with the Selection Tool (Figure 14-11b) and move it about the page.

Figure 14-11:
The Text and Selection tools.

a   b

5. Add a text effect.

Drop shadows is a really cool effect; it makes the text look like it's hovering over the page. Select the text. Click on Filters➪Light and Shadow➪Drop Shadow. Set the offsets both to 8 and the opacity to 80. Click OK. You finish up with a picture like the one in Figure 14-12.

Figure 14-12:
A finished piece of GIMP artwork.

6. Save your picture.

To save, click on File➪Save. You can now print it out and use it as part of a greeting card or whatever you like.

You can discover a lot about using GIMP just by experimenting. Try clicking on menus to see what's there. Open up some dialogue boxes and try dragging some of the sliders to see what happens. If you make a mistake, don't panic — just hit Ctrl+Z at the same time to undo your mistake.

If you want to experiment more hands-on with GIMP, look at some of these tutorial Web sites. There's loads of help out there:

- ✔ www.gimp.org/tutorials
- ✔ www.gimp-tutorials.com
- ✔ tutorialblog.org/gimp-tutorials

Getting the professional package with Photoshop

Adobe Photoshop (www.adobe.com/products/photoshop/photoshop) is so popular in the design community that its name has become a verb. You don't fix a photograph on your computer; you Photoshop it! Photoshop is the ultimate in image manipulation programs. With Photoshop, you can correct the color balance on your photographs, remove a pesky piece of litter from an otherwise beautiful picture, or use it to make new and original artwork.

The sheer power of Photoshop constantly amazes me. I often find myself thinking, "I wish I could do this" with Photoshop, and when I look, it turns out that I can. I use Photoshop for working with photographs for my paper models, as Figure 14-13 shows.

For in-depth, how-to information, check out the latest version of *Photoshop For Dummies* by Peter Bauer (Wiley).

GIMP and Photoshop are similar in many ways — you can even find a version of GIMP called GIMPshop that tries to make GIMP look and behave even more like Photoshop.

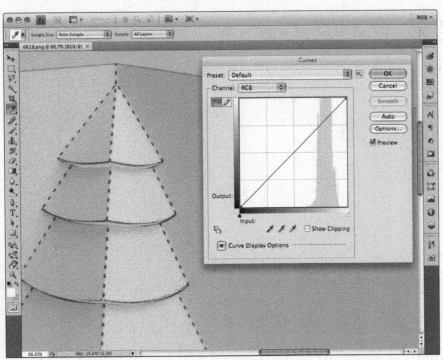

Figure 14-13:
Using
Photoshop
to work with
pictures.

Chapter 15

Making Some Extra Moolah by Selling Your Paper Creations

Making and designing paper-engineering projects is fun. You can send your pop-up cards to your friends and display your paper animations proudly on your window-sill, but there comes a time when you may want to reach a larger audience. Here's your chance to earn a little extra money by selling some of your paper creations.

In this chapter, I help you through the first steps of making money from your hobby. I look at ways to price and package your creations and how to get the most from your time and effort. I talk about selling at craft fairs — where and how to find them and how to make your stuff stand out. I also talk about selling online. Suddenly your ideas can have a worldwide audience.

Getting Ready for the Market

The better prepared you are, the more likely you are to find someone who wants to buy your products. This section focuses on what you need to do to get ready before you actually start selling your wares.

Getting the legal stuff in order

Presto change-o! If you're making and selling something for profit in the U.S., most states say you've automatically turned yourself into a business. That means you're required to do all the paperwork, registration, and tax-filing that comes with it. Expect to register as a business or get a temporary-business identification certificate, as well as apply for a permit to collect sales tax. On top of that, the government wants its share of your income, too, so you need to keep track of your profits.

Don't get on the wrong side of the law. If you're making money, then chances are you're going to need to pay some tax. Contact your state tax authorities or local business advisor to find out what the rules are and whether you're liable. Ask about the required paperwork and about collecting and filing taxes.

Starting small

The best way to start your paper-engineering business is to start small. By running an inexpensive stand at a local craft show, you can determine whether there's a demand for what you sell and whether you can expand in the future.

Do some research before you jump in over your head. If you're planning on selling at craft fairs (see the later section "Selling in Person: Hitting the Craft Fairs"), visit some of your local craft fairs and see what other people are doing. Spend some time watching what sells. Talk to the stall vendors about what sells and what doesn't. You'll often find that they're very helpful. Look for the following information as part of your research:

✔ **Pricing:** How do other vendors price their goods? How much are items similar to yours being sold for? (Check out the next section on pricing for more info.)

✔ **Packaging:** Look at how other people package their goods. Which packages look good and why? (See the "Packaging greeting cards and kits" section for helpful hints.)

I started off in a very small way. I was working as a teacher and was lucky enough to have a local publisher accept some of my paper-engineering designs. Over the next couple of years, I did a little designing in the evening when I wasn't busy with school work, and gradually over the years, I went from full-time teaching to half-time and then to one day a week. Finally, in 2000, I stopped teaching altogether and now work full time as a paper engineer. Baby steps.

Naming your price

You need to set your price at the right level. Too high, and no one buys your products; too low, and you end up losing money. When determining how much to charge for your different items, first find out how much your product cost you to make. Here's how:

1. **Figure out what you spent on materials for one product.**

   Write down the price of all the parts. Don't leave anything out, not even the little tiny things. Add the costs to give you a total cost.

2. **Determine the value of your time.**

   Carefully time how long each product takes to make or prepare. Decide how much money you want to make for each hour you work and then divide this number by the number of products you can make in an hour.

3. **Add the time cost to the materials cost to give you an overall cost per item.**

   If this price seems too high, you need to find ways of using either less time or cheaper materials to make your product.

Also look to see how similar items are selling and what your competition is charging. For example, if you're both selling a similar type of homemade greeting card but you're charging twice as much, examine why and see whether you can be more competitive in price.

Don't include sales tax as part of the marked price. Collecting sales tax on top of the marked price makes keeping the sales tax separate (so you can pay it to your state) that much easier. Check out your state's department of revenue for specifics about your state's sales tax.

Packaging greeting cards and kits

You may design lovely and fun paper-engineering masterpieces, but if your prospective buyers can't see what you're selling, then you're wasting your time and money. Ask people in marketing, and they'll tell you that the way you present and package your product can be the reason someone buys or doesn't buy your product. That's why packaging with care is important.

Having designed your range of perhaps ten different pop-up cards or several paper-animation kits, you can put some time in your evenings into making up some display packs. I do occasionally sell made-up models and finished paper sculptures, but most of the time what I sell are kits of parts (mostly marked-out card). People like to make up their own models, and putting together a kit involves less time for you.

So what do you need to do to package your cards or kits? Each display pack needs the following items:

- ✔ The greeting card or materials for the kit you designed
- ✔ An instruction sheet and a photo of the completed project (for kits)
- ✔ An envelope (for cards)
- ✔ A cellophane bag
- ✔ A price sticker
- ✔ A logo label like the one in Figure 15-1

Get a logo label printed at your local printer. Having a printer produce your label gives it a professional appearance. A properly printed logo should include information about who you are, your Web site address if you have one (check out the "Selling Online" section later in this chapter for more about having a Web site), and contact details so that customers who buy your products can come back for more.

Find your cellophane bags and envelopes first and then make greeting cards that fit them. Cellophane bags are usually available in craft stores, and you can purchase envelopes from the stationery store. Pack each greeting card, along with the envelope and the logo label.

Figure 15-1:
Design a logo label and get it professionally printed.

POP UP POWER!

Pop-up Greeting Card
by
Rob Ives

Broughton Moor, Maryport, Cumbria
CA15 7RU.
t. 01900 8154333
w. flying-pig.co.uk

Selling in Person: Hitting the Craft Fairs

A good place to start selling is at local craft fairs. These fairs take place all over the country. They happen year-round but are more frequent in the run-up to Christmas, when people are looking for gifts. Craft fairs usually take place over a weekend and run for one or two days. They're usually small, intimate events but are often well attended. You can usually find craft fairs at local churches, community centers, and so on, sometimes even within shopping centers or along the street.

Presenting your products at a craft fair gives you a chance to see whether customers are willing to part with their hard-earned cash in exchange for your marvelous creations. Selling at a fair is relatively cheap, and it gives you the chance to talk to your potential customers to find out what they like and what they don't.

If you're interested in going the craft fair route, this section helps you locate shows, explains what you need to prepare for the show, and gives advice on how to actually present and sell your goods.

Finding shows to attend

Craft fairs can take the form of juried art shows, Christmas bazaars, music festivals, fairs devoted to specific types of crafts, local food and cultural festivals, farmers' markets, and more. Before you can attend a craft fair, you need to find one. Here are a few ideas on how to track down the right show for you:

- ✔ **Look in your local press or listen to local radio for notices about upcoming events.** The local paper often has a section in or near the classifieds on upcoming events, and local radio stations sometimes have a public notice segment.

- ✔ **Check the notice board in your local arts and crafts shop.** Make sure you visit regularly so you can stay up-to-date with local events.

- ✔ **Contact local arts groups.** Find out about arts groups in the Yellow Pages or from your local library.

- ✔ **Visit local art galleries.** Proprietors of galleries often have an ear open for what's going on in the local arts and crafts scene.

- ✔ **While attending a craft fair, ask the sellers about other shows.** Fellow artists can point you to some of the best places to sell your projects.

After you find some shows to attend, spend a little time making sure that they're right for you. Ask the fair's registration folks the following questions before making your final decision:

- ✔ **What kind of show is it?** You won't be able to sell your pop-up cards at a ceramics show. Asking about what kinds of customers and vendors usually attend the show can also help you decide whether to bring your skull-and-crossbones pop-ups and leave the cute puppy and kitten ones at home.

✔ **Is the fair juried?** Juried shows let only some applicants in, based on the quality of their work and how many other vendors of the same type will be at the fair. These shows are often more expensive, but they're also more exclusive. At nonjuried shows, where registration is first-come, first-served, you may find yourself competing for customers with a lot of other greeting card sellers.

✔ **Is the show indoors or outdoors?** The choice is yours, but remember that an outdoor show in poor weather can be a miserable affair. Conversely, being out in the sun all day is great. If you choose to attend an outdoor fair, make sure you're prepared with an overhead awning.

✔ **How much is the fair registration?** You almost always have to pay to register your booth and sell your items, but some shows cost more than others. Make sure you don't have to pay more than you could earn. A typical craft fair costs less than $100 for a table.

✔ **What will be provided?** Some places provide tables for you, but many simply give you a certain amount of space and require you to bring all your display materials. Electricity may be available in a limited number of booths, usually for an extra fee.

✔ **When is the craft fair?** Before you part with your hard-earned cash, make sure you really are free for that date and that you'll be able to attend for the full length of the show. Know the setup and take-down times for the booths. You'll make yourself very unpopular if you leave the show early!

✔ **What's the last date for entry?** If you decide to go, make sure you get your application in on time.

✔ **What kind of paperwork do I need?** See whether you need to include your tax ID number or a copy of your sales tax permit when you send in your registration form. (See the earlier section "Getting the legal stuff in order.")

✔ **What's the cancellation policy?** You may have to cancel at the last minute due to an emergency. Check on what the cancellation and refund policy is to determine whether you can get your registration money refunded.

✔ **How much foot traffic have you had in recent years?** This info can give you an idea of how many people are likely to visit your stand. The more, the better.

Preparing for the craft fair

After you decide to attend a craft fair, you need to make sure you're ready. The most important step is to submit your application and application fee on time. The best shows can fill up quickly; it'd be a shame if you did all your show prep and then couldn't get a place. At this point, you'll probably be asked to part with your money.

Be prepared to write off the money you pay to register. Attending a show is no guarantee that people will buy your products. After you have your registration verified, ensure you're ready to show. The most important point I can say is to make sure you have enough merchandise to sell. There's nothing worse than getting a couple hours into your show and running out of stock so prospective buyers can't see what you're selling. Determining whether you have enough merchandise isn't easy, though. At your first show, you have to guess how much stock you need.

Keep accurate records of how many of each item you sell at each show; over time, you'll be able to make a more accurate prediction of how much merchandise you need to bring.

In addition to having enough merchandise, having a show box that includes everything you may need during the show is important. Over the years, I've added extra bits and pieces to the box as I've needed them. Here's a list of contents for your show box:

✔ **A folder containing all the show paperwork:** Going through the inevitable paperwork is easier if you have everything in one place.

✔ **Some postcards or simple leaflets that you can give away during the show:** These help to advertise your products. At a minimum, they should have your contact details and some sample pictures of your work.

✔ **A small paper-engineering toolbox:** This tool kit should contain your usual scissors, ruler, pencils and pens, and glue. You need these materials in case one of your projects needs a quick tune-up.

✔ **Heavy-duty scissors and box cutters:** These come in handy for all kinds of things, from opening boxes of stock to making minor modifications to your stand.

✔ **Fasteners:** Thumbtacks, staples, and some paper clips help you join things together. Many shows use fabric-covered wall units, and Velcro dots can let you easily fasten things to the wall.

✔ **Receipt book:** Bring this in case anyone needs a receipt for your sale. This book can also record everything you sell, which is a legal requirement.

✔ **Cash box with change:** This box is to keep all your earnings in. If you prefer, you can use a fanny pack for easy access to your change. Make sure you bring plenty of small bills and coins so you can make change.

✔ **Calculator:** Get a nice big one with a clear screen.

✔ **A toolbox containing a variety of tools:** Carry screwdrivers in various sizes, pliers, duct tape, elastic bands, string, and a hammer. These come in handy for setting up your stand, adjusting lighting, or keeping lighting wiring tidy.

✔ **A thermos and mug:** That way, you can take a hot drink with you.

✔ **A collapsible table to display your wares and a cover for the table:** Many fairs don't provide the tables, so you need to bring your own displays. As a table cover, a large piece of cloth does the job nicely. You need a piece of cloth that covers the top of your table and drapes right down to the floor at the front and sides of the table to keep your stock hidden. Make sure you give it a good iron and fold it neatly before you set off to the show.

Presenting your wares

When prospective buyers walk by your booth, you want to make a good first impression. Even if your merchandise is the most unique and interesting stuff on sale at the fair, you can turn away buyers with an unorganized and sloppy booth. Perception is key, so you want to display your wares in the best possible light (both figuratively and literally). Spend some time preparing the setup of your stand before you go to the show. If possible, try setting up your stand at home and get some feedback from some friends. Think about the way that shops encourage you to buy.

Keep the following do's and don'ts in mind as you set up your booth space:

✔ **Don't put all your stock on the table at once.** A huge pile of 100 of the same greeting card or model looks unsightly. Have two or three examples of each design out on the table and keep the rest of the stock safely out of the way under the table. The cloth covering on the table hides everything out of the way. After you sell something, replace it with a new item.

✔ **Do keep a binder with pictures of all your designs.** That way, if you run out of some stock items, you can still show them to prospective customers and take orders.

✔ **Do display some unpackaged items so viewers can see how they work.** If you're selling pop-ups, for instance, make sure you have an open sample for the potential customers to see.

✔ **Don't just lay your wares out on your table; try to use vertical space as well.** Take along some stands with you so you can have greeting cards and other items displayed at different heights.

If possible, add extra lighting. Some shows may have a board above your stand where you can add your own lights. I have a set of spotlights mounted on a piece of wood that I stick above my stand using duct tape. Lighting can really highlight your wares.

Digital downloads: The way of the future

If you're selling designs for paper models, then you really don't need to sell a printed model to the customers; what they need are the plans. Anyone who has access to your Web site almost always has access to a printer. By selling digital plans for paper models, you can send your ideas to anyone, anywhere in the world, instantly. You can do it whether you're there or not. It's a truly satisfying feeling to check your e-mail in the morning and find that you've sold several of your designs to people from as far apart as Japan and South America! I think that this really is the way of the future.

Selling digital downloads is surprisingly easy:

1. **Create your design on the computer and save your design as a PDF file if possible.**

Make sure that you have the © symbol somewhere in the file along with your name and the year. Use one of the software packages I outline in Chapter 14.

2. **Sign up for a suitable download manager.**

I use E-junkie (www.e-junkie.com), but others are available. Download managers generally charge a monthly fee based on how many products you want to offer for sale and/or the size of your files.

3. **Upload the file you created onto the download manager's Web site.**

4. **Follow the download manager's instructions to add a "buy" button to your Web site.**

5. **Sit back and wait for the money to come in!**

Selling at your show

You didn't pay a registration fee just to sit at your booth and do some people-watching. To seal the deal, you want to develop your selling skills and show prospective buyers why your merchandise makes the best gifts or additions to their homes. Keep the following suggestions in mind to help you make the sale:

✔ **Be courteous to customers and other vendors.** Everyone likes a smile and cheerful hello when shopping.

✔ **Let customers look without interrupting them.** Be ready to answer any questions they have and to talk to people about your products, but let them initiate the conversation.

✔ **Don't ignore them.** Don't bury your head in a book or spend your time filling in your sales book. Don't ever sit with your back to your customers. Always be ready so that a prospective customer can catch your eye.

✔ **Listen to the comments people make about your products.** You can get some good feedback on your creations simply by keeping your ears open.

✔ **Put on a demonstration if you have a quiet moment at your stand.** Get your scissors out and start making one of your kits. Doing so attracts interest and a crowd.

✔ **If customers are interested, talk about what you do.** You may feel like you're repeating yourself, but remember it's new to them.

Selling Online

The Internet is a great place for selling your paper creations. The wonderful thing about selling online is that with a little skill, you can set up a Web site to sell your models and give the impression of being a big professional operation, even if you're just operating out of a couple of boxes and a laptop from your front room.

Here are a few ways you can try to sell your paper creations on the Net:

✔ **Sell on eBay.** Setting up a simple shop within the framework of eBay is easy. You can start selling just one thing and build up from there. Over time, you can build up a following. When you add a new item to your eBay shop, your previous customers and people who are interested will be automatically notified.

✔ **Start a blog.** A *blog,* short for *Weblog,* is a kind of online diary, but it can be so much more than this. You can use it to attract attention to your products, and using some simple payment-management tools such as PayPal (www.paypal.com), you can set up a shop within your blog to sell online. One of the many advantages of a blog is that in its simplest form, it's completely free. Check out *Blogging For Dummies,* 2nd edition, by Susannah Gardner and Shane Birley (Wiley) for more information.

✔ **Set up a Web site.** When you get really serious, set up a proper Web site. Setting up a Web site isn't that difficult, and you can use it to sell digital downloads (see the nearby sidebar). Check out *Building a Web Site For Dummies,* 3rd edition, by David A. Crowder (Wiley).

✔ **Sell your models or greeting cards on one of the craft-based Web sites.** The best known of these is probably Etsy (www.etsy.com).

Part V
The Part of Tens

In this part . . .

Like all *For Dummies* books, this one finishes with
the Part of Tens. What *For Dummies* book would be
complete without it? Here, I give you ten tips on avoiding
pitfalls and on making the most of your paper-engineering
projects. I also name ten ways you can play around with
models and improve your design skills.

Chapter 16

Ten Tips for Perfect Paper Projects

In This Chapter
▶ Getting ready
▶ Practicing good techniques
▶ Keeping your tools in working condition

*Y*ou need to avoid some pitfalls if you want to do some excellent paper engineering. Here are my top ten tips for making sure your projects go smoothly. Follow them, and you'll be proud to sign your name on your latest creations and explain why you've spent so much time in your workshop lately.

Read the Directions

Whether you're making paper-engineering projects from this book or from other sources, always make sure you read the instructions from start to finish before beginning. There's nothing worse than getting to the end of making a model and only then coming across the warning about not gluing the thingy to the whatsit! Reading the directions also gives you a general idea of how everything fits together, which can be helpful when you're making individual pieces.

You need both the text and the diagrams to get the most from the directions. Use the pictures in the instructions to help you, and make sure you read the text as well.

Stay Clean and Organized

Put some effort into keeping your workspace (mostly) clean and organized. You'll be able to work more safely and efficiently, and you won't end up with random bits of paper glued to your project — or scattered around the house. Here are some ways to keep your paper projects under control:

✔ **Store your tools.** Make sure you keep your paper-engineering tools, especially the sharp ones, in a safe place. Keep them is a closable box while you're not using them. When you are using them, get in the habit of keeping your tools away from the edge of your desk, somewhere safe from little hands.

✔ **Organize your materials.** Use a chest of drawers, box lids functioning as trays, and other storage containers to give you easy access to paper and embellishments and to keep them from getting damaged.

✔ **Dispose of scrap paper.** To keep your workspace and the paper you're using tidy, have a small box or dish on your desk to keep your paper offcuts in. As you cut out your model, put the offcuts into the dish so they're all in one place. If the offcuts are large, quickly snip them up so they fit in the dish. When you finish your work for the day, simply empty the offcut dish into the trash or recycling bin — no need to collect lots of bits from all over the room!

✔ **Wash your hands.** Nothing spoils your paper model more than dirty fingerprints. Always make sure your hands are clean before you start your paper-engineering project.

✔ **Try to keep your model as clean as possible by keeping your tools clean.** Before you start with your latest project, clean your ruler with soap and water and dry it thoroughly. This is especially important if you've been using a felt-tipped pen with your ruler.

Check out Chapter 3 for more pointers on keeping an organized and clean workspace.

Use the Best Materials Available

Always try to use quality paper and card for your paper-engineering projects. Usually the best materials are the most expensive. If you're not sure about the quality of the card or the paper you're buying, ask the shop assistant for some advice.

The difference in the look and feel of the finished product is well worth the few extra cents you need to spend. Paper is a relatively cheap material; even pricey paper isn't out of the reach of most pockets.

Mark on the Back of Your Paper

If possible, do your marking on the back of your paper. That way, you won't have to rub out your pencil lines.

If you mark the back of your sheet, you need to reverse your picture so that it'll be the right way around when you flip it over. Chapter 4 can give you tips on reversing images you trace.

If you can't mark the back of your paper, make sure you use a soft pencil (2B), and don't press so hard that you make a dent in the paper.

Pay Attention to Accuracy

To make the best paper model you can, you need to be accurate. Carelessness can lead to a model with gaps in it, a pop-up that doesn't fold flat, or a mechanism that doesn't move. Here are some ways to make sure you stay accurate as you measure, mark, and cut your card:

✔ **Measuring:** When you measure a piece of paper, make sure you put the zero mark of the ruler exactly on the edge of the page; then use a super sharp pencil for marking where your measurement goes.

✔ **Drawing:** When you're drawing a line across a piece of paper, you need to measure out two points, one at each end of the line. Use these points to align your ruler and draw your line.

✔ **Cutting:** After you mark out where you want to make your cut, try to cut the guideline in half. There should be a fine line of pencil on either side of your cut.

For more marking and cutting techniques, turn to Chapter 4.

Score Your Crease Lines

A crisp crease line makes a model look good. The best way to ensure sharp creases is to score before you fold. Scoring is a simply a matter of making a dent in the paper where you want the fold to be. Here's the simplest way to score:

1. **Line your ruler up with the line you're scoring.**

2. **Without pressing too hard, run the point of an open pair of scissors along the line.**

   The scissors point should dent the card instead of cutting it. If your scissors are too sharp, try a different pair.

After you score your card or paper to perfection, folding it crisply and accurately is easy. If you want to really finish off the crease, then fold it over and run a fingernail along its length.

Take Care of Your Good Scissors

Your good scissors are sacred! Don't use them for cutting roses in the garden or for getting stones out of horses' hooves — you don't want to gum them up or nick the blades. Use your scissors only for cutting paper and card, and make sure that everyone else treats them well, too. If other people want to use your scissors, make sure they know the rules.

For best results when cutting, you need to use sharp scissors. Fortunately, scissors keep their edges much longer than craft knives do. Finding someone who can sharpen your scissors for you can be difficult, so after scissors lose their edge, it's often easier just to get another pair. However, if you have a high quality pair of scissors, you can go to the fabric or hardware store and ask for some recommendations about hiring professional sharpeners. Sharpening usually costs several dollars. Some manufacturers even let you send the scissors back for sharpening.

Replace Dull Craft Knife Blades

One of the problems with scalpel-style craft knives is that the blades last only a limited amount of time. It's surprising how just cutting out some paper and card can take the edge off your super sharp knife. When you use dull blades, your cuts aren't as crisp. You also have to push harder to make a cut, which puts you in a pretty dicey situation if the blade slips.

You need to replace your blades quite often. In as little as 30 minute of cutting, your blade loses its edge. Make sure you keep plenty of spare blades on hand.

When replacing your dull blades, remember that they're still sharp enough to do some serious damage. Dispose of the blades carefully. I always wrap the used blades from my knives in a piece of paper folded over several times and then hold the whole package shut with some sticky tape. Only then do I consign the whole package to the bin. Don't forget that even though you've thrown something into the trash, it may still pose a risk to people or animals. (Check out Chapter 4 for more safety tips.)

Use the Right Amount of White School Glue

Most of your paper-engineering work requires you to use white school glue. This glue is surprisingly strong, so don't use more than you need. If you use too much glue, the joint takes ages to dry, and excess glue can make the paper go soggy or attract dirt.

A joint well made using white school glue is actually stronger than the surrounding paper because the glue holds the fibers of the paper together. Here's how to use the right amount of white school glue:

1. **Put a small amount of glue into a small container with a resealable lid.**

   An old jam jar works well, or you can use a cleaned-out fish food container.

2. **Dip your glue spreader into your glue.**

   A wooden coffee stirrer works well as a glue spreader.

3. **Wipe most of the glue off the spreader on the side of the glue container.**

4. **Spread on a thin layer of glue.**

   When you spread glue onto the paper you're sticking, the layer needs to be thin enough that you can see right through it. With white school glue, you need to apply glue only to one surface.

Keep Your Projects Dry

Preventing your paper-engineering projects and models from getting wet is essential for them to work properly. You're probably not going to take your masterpiece out in the rain (if you do, it'll turn to mush in no time). However, you also need to consider other ways your project can get wet while you're working on it.

Don't use too much glue, and if you're using water-based paint or pens, make sure you don't soak the paper. If possible, use solvent-based pens or try making your models out of precolored paper or card. Check out Chapter 4 for proper gluing and coloring techniques.

Chapter 17

Ten Ways to Develop Your Design Skills

In This Chapter

▶ Making new designs

▶ Varying existing models

▶ Expanding your options

Using a kit or someone else's patterns and templates is just the beginning. When you understand how to make paper pop up or move or fold in a certain way, you're ready to turn your paper-engineering workshop into a design studio. Whether you want to modify someone else's pattern or create a design from scratch, taking a few chances can personalize your project and make it great. In this chapter, I give you ten tips for improving your design skills.

Carry a Notebook and Sketch It Out

You never know when you're going to get hit with a good idea, so carry a notebook with you at all times and use it to jot down your ideas. You don't need to draw a masterpiece — just something to remind you what your idea was. When you come up with an idea, don't pause to think about whether it's good enough; just write it down or sketch it. You can decide later whether you want to go any further with that plan. Check out Chapter 13 for more about using a notebook to record your ideas.

Do a Little Aimless Construction

From scoring the perfect crease to designing your next pop-up masterpiece, the thing that will keep you improving is practice. However, you don't need to spend all that practice time drawing, cutting, or scoring boring rows of straight lines.

Experiment and play around as you practice your paper-engineering techniques. It's worth spending time just cutting, folding, and sticking with no particular aim in mind. Think of it as paper-engineering doodling. You never know when you'll come up with a solution to a problem or a new model idea. Keep a supply of paper and glue on hand so you can keep trying out new ideas and experimenting with designs.

Study Machines and Mechanisms

Paper engineering uses the same principles as all branches of engineering. You can discover loads that you can apply to paper engineering by taking things apart and seeing how they work. Look out for bits of machinery such as old video recorders that aren't being used anymore; just get your screwdrivers out and take the recorder apart. Look at how the parts fit together and see whether you understand how the machine works. Think about how you can use these mechanisms in your paper engineering.

Don't take apart TVs or computer monitors, and never take apart machines that are plugged in. You really don't want to risk an electric shock.

Look for Inspiration from Other Artists

You can find out a lot from other paper engineers. By talking to other paper engineers, reading their books, and experimenting with their projects, you can pick up some great ideas and tips. Look at how they make things, what materials they use, and how they fasten things together.

You can also discover a lot from other kinds of artists, not just paper engineers. Notice how painters use colors and shapes. Watch how potters use 3D forms. Keep a notebook of examples of artwork that you like or admire, and refer to it when designing your new models.

The Web can be a fantastic source of inspiration. Peruse some of these craft and design sites for some general art ideas:

- www.craftzine.com
- www.etsy.com
- www.instructables.com

Start with a Simple Design

When you're creating a new model, start with a simple idea for a simple design. Aim for simple success first and then build on it. For example, one of my models features a row of chickens pecking at the ground in succession. My first model was of a single chicken, just to get the mechanism working. After I got it working, I moved on to the model with four chickens.

After you get more comfortable with simple projects, you can always go on to make your idea more complex in the future. Starting complicated can be discouraging.

Be Open to New Methods

When you experiment with paper engineering, you find that there are often many ways of achieving the same effect, be it planning ways to make your pop-up pop up or how to apply color to your model. For example, when you're designing paper animations in which characters move up and down, you can use cams or crank sliders — both have similar effects. There's no one correct way. Be open to different approaches and new techniques, and you may find ways to make projects more efficiently or how to get just the effect you want. (For more on cams and crank sliders, see Chapters 10 and 12.)

Experiment with Different Weights of Paper

Getting the correct paper thickness (weight) is important. If you use paper that's too thin, you'll have a model that flops apart and doesn't feel good in the hand. Conversely, if you use paper or card that's too heavy, then the moving parts of your model won't move as easily as they might. As so often in engineering of all sorts, getting the correct weight is a balancing act.

Design your model, make it, and see how it works. If the parts are too stiff, try a lighter paper; if everything is too floppy, try a heavier paper. Try to keep a range of paper weights in your paper store so you can experiment when designing. (Check out Chapter 2 for more info on paper.)

Try Creating a Model in a Different Size

If you've made a model that you're happy with, why not try making the same thing on a different scale? Sometimes making a model bigger or smaller is all that it needs to change it from being good to being great. If you created your design on a computer, then changing the size is simply a matter of using the scale tool. Otherwise, try multiplying all your measurements by a fixed number — try one and a half times larger or two-thirds the size.

If you change the size of a model, you may need to change the weight of the paper as well. Use lighter paper for smaller models, heavier paper for bigger models.

Collect New Types of Materials

When you're shopping, look out for new types of paper and for new things that you can use as embellishments. By considering nontraditional items, you can expand your design options.

You can start looking at local arts and crafts stores, but I also suggest you look in other places. Look for sticker packs at a large discount store. Experiment with some types of dried food to embellish your greeting cards. Always be on the lookout for new items. When you find them, keep your findings neatly packed so you can easily look through the materials and find what you need.

Don't Give Up

Making paper-engineering projects is just like any other task in life. Sometimes you do okay; other times you may fail and need to start over. No matter what you do, don't get discouraged. It's a cliché, but practice really does make perfect. You may well find that the very first pop-up that you design doesn't work quite as well as you hoped. Break down the steps you took, see where you went wrong, and then correct it. If that doesn't work, start over and take your time. No matter what, don't quit. The more you practice, the better you'll get.

Sharing your successes can help you stay motivated. Put your finished project out on the mantelpiece or on top of the TV for all to see. You'll be delighted by the appreciative interest you get from your family and from visitors to your home. Take photographs of your creations as you make them so you have a record; then, when you have the time, make a blog on the Internet to share your ideas with the whole world!

Index